PRAISE FOR *FLIRTING WITH FAITH*

"I love authors with attitude—that's why Anne Lamott is high on my favorites list. Now even higher is the new voice of Joan Ball. Her splendor of rendering life in the spirit is unmatched. Open this book up anywhere, and it grabs you everywhere."

—Leonard Sweet, author of *So Beautiful* and more,
professor at Drew University and George Fox University

"Even Joan Ball wouldn't have believed the story—successful New York publicist gets blindsided by a supernatural smack-down—had it not happened to her. Every part of Joan's faith journey reeks of authenticity. And it's not just the story of *Flirting with Faith* that will keep you turning the pages. Joan's voice is one of the most original to come along in years. She's bold and brash and filled with a kind of wide-eyed wonder that could only come from someone who has been 'struck Christian.'"

—Stan Jantz, bestselling author of *I'm Fine with God . . .
It's Christians I Can't Stand* and more, cofounder of ConversantLife.com

"In a culture where far too many people are dismissive or completely indifferent when it comes to faith, it's refreshing to see it dealt with in such an honest and authentic fashion. *Flirting with Faith* is a roadmap on the often perilous and sometime exhilarating journey to discover eternity. Joan Ball reminds us that encountering real faith will change everything."

—Phil Cooke, filmmaker and author of
Branding Faith and *The Last TV Evangelist*

"In *Flirting with Faith* Joan Ball reveals the scarred soul of an avowed atheist who found herself unexpectedly God-smacked. Fellow spiritual oddballs will delight in the discovery that, while they may be unique, they're not alone. Through Ball's story, they can find another broken believer who walked a crooked spiritual path that eventually wound its way to God."

—Becky Garrison, religious satirist and author of *Jesus Died for This?*

"What Joan Ball gives us here is a conversion story that St. Paul himself could have written. Spiced with humor and told with all the natural storytelling skills of a true writer, *Flirting* is, above all else, a dramatic, moving, and overwhelmingly credible confession of faith by one woman who never, ever meant to be converted. God apparently thought otherwise, and the resulting story will rejoice both your heart and your mind."

—Phyllis Tickle, founding editor of the religion department of *Publishers Weekly* and author of more than two dozen books, including *The Words of Jesus* and *The Great Emergence*

"*Flirting with Faith* is so much more than a personal memoir. It's a vulnerable, spiritual journey. With each word, Joan Ball invites us to take a step into her heart, where we see the beauty of transformation and the freedom of grace."

—Anne Jackson, author of *Mad Church Disease* and *Permission to Speak Freely*

"Storyteller Joan Ball has found a way into my mind, heart, and soul with the beautifully written tale of her accidental fall into the lap of her loving Savior. I tell stories in three-minute blurbs wrapped up in a melody that I pray get stuck in someone's head. What Joan has managed to do with *Flirting with Faith* is to create a story that has escaped my lips to countless friends as easily as the catchiest pop hook. This story will remind you that you are ultimately not in control, and when you finally accept that, your own flirting with faith will turn into a full-blown romance."

—Carlos Whittaker, Integrity Music recording artist and blogger at RagamuffinSoul.com

"At once feisty and contemplative, Joan Ball's *Flirting with Faith* more than flirts: She dances with both faith and doubt, while being unflinchingly honest each step of the way. Her authentic wrestling will confound skeptics, challenge believers, and comfort those who mourn."

—Makoto Fujimura, artist, author of *Refractions*

Flirting *with* Faith

JOAN BALL

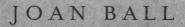

Flirting *with* Faith

MY SPIRITUAL JOURNEY

FROM ATHEISM *to a* FAITH-FILLED LIFE

HOWARD BOOKS
A DIVISION OF SIMON & SCHUSTER, INC.

New York Nashville London Toronto Sydney

Published by Howard Books, a division of Simon & Schuster, Inc.
1230 Avenue of the Americas, New York, NY 10020

The names and other identifying characteristics of certain people in this book have been changed.

Flirting with Faith © 2010 Joan Ball

All rights reserved, including the right to reproduce this book or portions thereof in any form whatsoever. For information, address Howard Subsidiary Rights Department, 1230 Avenue of the Americas, New York, NY 10020.

In association with the literary agency of Rosenbaum & Associates Literary Agency, Inc.

Library of Congress Control Number: 2010008483

ISBN 978-1-4391-4987-4
ISBN 978-1-4391-5536-3 (ebook)

10 9 8 7 6 5 4 3 2 1

HOWARD and colophon are registered trademarks of Simon & Schuster, Inc.

Manufactured in the United States of America

For information regarding special discounts for bulk purchases, please contact Simon & Schuster Special Sales at 1-866-506-1949 or business@simonandschuster.com.

The Simon & Schuster Speakers Bureau can bring authors to your live event. For more information or to book an event, contact the Simon & Schuster Speakers Bureau at 1-866-248-3049 or visit our website at www.simonspeakers.com.

Edited by Philis Boultinghouse
Interior design by Jaime Putorti
Photography/illustrations by Scott Cornell

The scripture quoted in chapter 6 (Ephesians 5:22–24) is taken from *The Holy Bible, New International Version* ®. Copyright © 1973, 1978, 1984 by International Bible Society. Used by permission of Zondervan Publishing House. All rights reserved. The scripture quoted in chapter 1x (Revelation 19:11–16) is taken from *The Message*. Copyright © 1993, 1994, 1995, 1996, 2000, 2001, 2002. Used by permission of NavPress Publishing Group. The scripture quoted in chapter 15 (Romans 5:3–5) is taken from the *New American Standard Bible*®, copyright © 1960, 1962, 1963, 1968, 1971, 1972, 1973, 1975, 1977, 1995 by The Lockman Foundation. Used by permission. www.Lockman.org.

In loving memory of Joan and Warren Burger

CONTENTS

ACKNOWLEDGMENTS

This book would not be possible without dozens of people who've made the time to listen, read, and guide this story as it was lived and written. Your kindness, patience, acceptance, and skepticism inspired me to learn to tell a genuine story— something I will spend the rest of my life learning to do better.

Special thanks to Howard Books editor Philis Boulting-house, agent Bucky Rosenbaum, Conversantlife.com founder Stan Jantz, editor Nicole Symmonds, former editor Patton Dodd from Beliefnet.com, and *In Touch Weekly* editor Erin Geishen for taking a chance on an unknown, no-platform writer in a very competitive publishing environment. I pray it was a risk worth taking.

Thanks to Brother Bernard Delcourt and the community at Holy Cross Monastery in West Park, New York, for your hospitality, generosity, and guidance, as well as to the owners and staff at each of the cafés in Warwick, New York, where I spent countless hours drinking cappuccinos, writing, studying, and thinking: The Tuscan Cafe, Carriage Path Café, Caffe a la Mode, La Petit Cuisine, and Charlotte's Tea Room.

Thanks to Nancy Rawlinson and the Village Natural Crew (Catherine Hull, Emily Epstein, Tony Longo, and Sally Donaldson) for your input and critique, and to my good friends Jackie and Ken Straut, Linda Mensch, Andrea Gross Colman,

Linda Kurtz, and others who read early drafts, prayed, and encouraged me along the way.

Sincerest thanks to my family. To my brothers, Dean, Danny, and Warren; my sister, Jennifer; and their families, who came to my rescue in the darkest years. To my in-laws, Darioleta and Jose Dominguez; Dary and Jack Politoski and their children, Victoria, Natalie, and Matt for your love and support. And finally, to Martin, Andrew, Kelsey, and Ian for making room for me to become the woman I am meant to be, even when it wasn't easy. I love you.

Flirting *with* Faith

Struck

Thirty-seven is way too young to be having a heart attack, I thought, resting my hand on my chest and struggling to catch my breath. *I'm sure it's nothing*.

But somewhere deep inside I knew I was lying to myself. Although I was a firm believer in mind over matter, my attempts to will away the waves of nausea and shortness of breath were failing miserably.

As my stoic resolve began to dissolve into genuine concern, *I think there might actually be something wrong with me*.

I looked at my watch, then over my shoulder into the serious-looking faces of forty or fifty strangers scattered in little clumps throughout the massive, mostly empty main sanctuary of a church we'd been attending for about a month. These clean-cut, well-manicured families in their suits and dresses and sensible shoes were way too straitlaced for my taste. In fact, they perfectly embodied the stereotype of church folks I'd carried along on my spiritual (and sometimes not so spiritual) journey from staunch atheism to recovery-based, power-greater-than-myself pseudo-agnosticism. They appeared boring and predictable; I saw nothing of myself in these people, and I was confident that their conception of Jesus as God was a farce.

Despite my growing concern over the pressure in my chest, I sat motionless, proud enough to choose the anonymity of the pew over creating a scene with a quick exit.

———————

Of course, this begs the question: What was I doing there in the first place?

Faith aside, church and a nice brunch made for a surprisingly relaxing Sunday-morning routine that offset nicely the insane pace we managed to maintain Monday through Saturday. And since the kids liked meeting their friends there, it seemed like a benign sacrifice of an hour in exchange for some quality family-bonding time.

Even so, I didn't really trust these church people. There was something about their unwavering propriety that I was sure amounted to little more than a thin disguise for a subtle yet palpable wariness of "outsiders." Maybe it was the body language or the tone of their voices, but I always came away with the distinct sense that our presence was more tolerated than welcomed. Sure, they did all the right things. The smiles, hellos, and "how-was-your-week's" were delivered perfectly, as if on cue. But, in the white space between the pleasantries, there was this underlying *something* that I couldn't quite put my finger on.

It was kind of like a friend hosting a party who meets you at the door with a pleasant "Come on in. Make yourself at home. Can I get you a drink?" while shooting daggers at the husband she was fighting with as you pulled up the driveway. The words and actions say welcome, but you can't help but feel otherwise.

Seven years in addiction recovery had conditioned me to believe that the newcomer—on the wagon or still drinking—is always the most important person in the room. This made the perceived lack of warmth distasteful enough that I thought it best to maintain a polite distance, just to be safe. That said, at this point in my life the polite distance suited me just fine. In fact, the protective cordiality on both sides allowed my husband, Martin, our three kids, and me finally, after nearly two years of halfhearted church shopping, to consider this a place where we might hang our spiritual hats.

I probably wouldn't have been at church at all if I'd not married Martin six years earlier. When we met, in 1992, I was a single mother and a rabid atheist. More than that, my most potent venom was reserved for theists of the Christian persuasion. I've since been told that this brand of anti-theism is frequently born in bad experiences with the church or parochial school, but I was raised without any of that religious baggage.

Although my parents had grown up Roman Catholic, they abandoned the practice before I started grade school. So, coming from what could best be called a pull-yourself-up-by-your-bootstraps secular environment, I'd pieced together my own personal philosophy on religion and faith. In my view, people who embraced God and religion were emotionally, physically, or intellectually weak and unable to carry themselves through life on their own. This elaborate ruse called faith provided them with an external construct to prop them up. A fantasy scaffolding that I was smart enough and strong enough to avoid.

> *"In my view, people who embraced God and religion were emotionally, physically, or intellectually weak and unable to carry themselves through life on their own."*

Although I vehemently disparaged believers, certain people or groups were paradoxically excluded from my disdain. My devout Catholic grandmother and others in my mother's family fell into this category, as did anyone who embraced a spiritual path that I perceived to be cooler than Christianity—which included almost every religion or faith tradition on earth that *wasn't* Christianity. I have to admit that their pardon was based on random criteria that made neither logical nor theological sense. Naturally, Martin—at the time a Bible-believing, Pentecostal-church-attending Christian—was exempt from my ire. But that was mainly because he was sexy, played guitar, and rarely talked about God unless someone else brought it up.

I was like one of those aggressively discriminatory people who hate blacks or whites or gays, yet has one of those "friends who is different" from the stereotype. Somehow, the people I loved and respected were excused from my considerable contempt for Christians, yet I never disbanded my theory that faith was an illusion. It was this kind of convoluted mental calculus that allowed me to agree to a church wedding to Martin in 1996, and that fueled my sporadic church attendance—devoid of Christian faith—for the years that followed.

Surprisingly, in those months before and after we were married, I actually came to like going to church. There was something about the rhythm of doing the same thing once a week, every week, that was . . . I don't know . . . *comforting.* Like playing house as a child.

And I got pretty good at playing church.

We went on Sundays and took the kids to a family program on Wednesdays. I even stepped in as a substitute Sunday-school teacher once or twice, which was really weird, since I couldn't have answered even the simplest questions about the faith with any depth or accuracy if I'd been asked. Thankfully my students were four- and five-year-olds, and I'd been given a pretty thorough syllabus, so no one ever called my bluff. I probably could have continued attending church like that forever—a polite, clandestine agnostic—and no one would have been the wiser. But then we decided to move.

————————

When we settled into our house in Warwick, a rural suburb of New York City, church became an inconvenience. The longer drive from our new house to church got real old, real quick and it didn't take long for us to realize that losing twenty minutes of sleep to make it to church on time required a greater sacrifice than we were willing to make. After a couple months of setting the clock, overusing the snooze button, and vowing to "try again next week," we figured we'd try to find a new church in Warwick. When our admittedly halfhearted search for a new place failed, we gave church a little rest. Surely Martin's Jesus would understand that we were busy people with busy lives. Sunday was the only day that we were guaranteed a chance to sleep in. This omnipotent God had to know we worked hard to balance our careers, the kids' activities, and the house all week and that we wanted—no, we *deserved*—a little extra sleep on Sunday mornings.

What we thought would be a short hiatus from church lasted about two years, until our daughter, Kesley, who was thirteen at the time, asked a plaintive question.

"Mom? Do you think we'll ever go to church again?"

I had never gone to church as a kid, but I do remember what I was up to when I was thirteen. If I had a kid who was actually *asking* to go to church, I figured I should probably listen.

"Sure, Kels," I said, trying to sound enthusiastic. "We'll go back soon."

—————

So, as quickly as we'd abandoned the Sunday-morning church routine, we reinstated it.

The routine was simple and predictable. We'd start out calm and quiet. Andrew and Ian, who were fourteen and five at the time, were the early risers. They'd wake up and make their way down to the basement family room, where they'd stretch out on facing couches and watch TV or play video games. Kelsey, who was a little slower and a lot grumpier in the morning, usually slept in until the last possible minute. Martin and I fell somewhere in the middle. We'd set the clock for far earlier than either of us intended to wake up and hit the snooze (love that snooze) before lounging in bed, talking or reading (or whatever . . .), until we'd lingered just long enough to get to church almost on time.

Now, if you ask me, being almost on time for anything is far worse than being completely late. Completely late makes it easier to resort to a simple, more relaxing Plan B, like "Let's just sleep in" or "How about breakfast instead?" Being almost on time, on the other hand, held out a faint but real hope that, despite evidence to the contrary, Plan A may still be achievable. Almost on time got our competitive juices flowing and opened the door to chaos. It told us that, if we hustled, we might just make up the time—even if it meant tormenting ourselves and our children and ruining an otherwise peaceful morning. Martin and I took the bait every time.

"Kelsey, can you *please* finish getting ready and help your brother find his shoes?" I'd shout up from the bottom of the two-story foyer.

"You can't wear that shirt, it's dirty. Go change." Martin would say as he abruptly intercepted Andrew in the kitchen.

Then I'd snap at our youngest as he followed me from room to room, holding a hundred trading cards and a shoe. "No, Ian, you cannot bring your Pokémon cards. Go ask Kelsey to help you find your other shoe."

And finally, as if playing a role in a recurring nightmare, Martin would call from the back deck, "If you guys are not in the car in two minutes . . ."

Getting two adults, two teenagers, and a five-year-old showered, dressed, and out the door of a three-story house with three bathrooms shouldn't be that difficult. And yet somehow it always was. So much for the nice, relaxing family morning.

Eventually, we'd pile into our SUV and back down the cobblestone driveway, catching a glimpse of our picture-postcard, red brick center-hall colonial as we went.

That Sunday morning in 2003 was no different.

"Martin, can I have my sunglasses?" I asked, turning down the cul-de-sac straight into the surprisingly strong spring sunshine.

"Where are they?" he said as he leaned down to rifle through my bigger-than-necessary bag.

"They should be in the inside pocket," I said, hitting the gas, checking my makeup in the rearview mirror, and handing him my glasses in one unconscious and mindlessly dangerous motion.

He took my black-framed, cat-eye glasses and handed me a pair of dark Jackie-Os that set off my shoulder-length blond hair and monochromatic black outfit, completing the New York urban-chic style that I was trying hard to make look easy.

I looked down at the digital display—*9:54 A.M.* With six minutes to drive five minutes across town, we were still in the game. I made a quick right out of the cul-de-sac, rolled through a couple of stop signs, and turned into the parking lot as the church bells sounded the last deep *doooong*. Breathing a sigh of relief, we hit our seats just in time for the organist to play the intro to the first hymn.

Yes, I thought, *there's nothing like landing on the right side of almost on time.*

As the notes boomed out of the enormous antique pipe organ and the robe-clad choir fought a losing battle to find the right key, I found myself looking up at the arched stained-glass windows that flanked the massive stone church. Someone had once told me that the panels were museum quality, designed and constructed by Tiffany & Co. I wouldn't be surprised if it were true. They were amazing. Intricate patterns of metal and glass joined to form complex jewel-toned images of Jesus and his crew that exploded when backlit by the sun. I followed the colored beams as they cascaded through well-defined images of faces, bodies, and crosses into an impromptu dance of color that shifted on the floor as if projected by a giant, priceless kaleidoscope.

> *"With six minutes to drive five minutes across town, we were still in the game."*

I could always appreciate the majestic beauty of a church or cathedral. It was all that religion that happened inside that turned me off. *I wonder how much you could get for those things at Sotheby's*, I thought as I turned my attention forward, where a boyish-looking man was calling the congregation to order. He wore a long white robe with a purple sash, the standard uniform for what the church people referred to as the traditional service.

This pastor, whom I will call Pastor Thomas, was about the same age as Martin and me—somewhere in his mid- to late thirties. Despite the fact that he was a little geeky, he seemed nice enough from a distance. We'd only spoken to him once or twice: brief, *nice-to-see-you-back-again, so-nice-to-be-back* conversations as we left the church. We might have avoided these rather awkward exchanges altogether were it not his custom to stand at the back door of the church sanctuary at the end of the service. It was like the receiving line at a wedding: people making their way down aisles at the left, right, and center of the enormous room, converging at the back into a human traffic jam.

"Before we get started," Pastor Thomas announced with a broad smile on his face, "Mary Rooney and her son Jason [not their real names] are going to be accepted as new members of our congregation." Apparently, anyone can go to church, but becoming a member took it to the next level. I just wasn't sure what that next level looked like.

I almost applauded when the two of them stood up, but caught myself, forgetting that the people here never clapped. Even when singers did a fantastic duet or solo . . . nothing. No one else seemed to mind, but I found that pregnant pause while the musicians cleared their music and returned to their seats in silence to be distractingly awkward. One day I made the mistake of using the no-clapping thing as fodder for pre-service small talk with one of the women who seemed to be involved in a number of church activities.

"I almost applauded when the two of them stood up, but caught myself, forgetting that the people here never clapped."

"Why is it," I asked, "that no one ever claps for the singers or musicians?"

She made no attempt to hide her disdain for my question as she said curtly, "This is a church, not a concert."

As Mary and her elementary-school-age son came to their feet, I wondered whether they were alone because of a divorce, if her husband had died, or if she had just chosen to have a child on her own. Whatever the circumstances, they reminded me of how difficult it had been to be a single mother and how lucky Andrew, Kelsey, and I were to have Martin in our lives. Once Ian was born, our new family was complete.

Pastor Thomas made his way across the stage (I think there's a more formal name for it, but it looked like a stage to me) and opened a huge book that sat on a quartersawn oak pedestal. Then, without speaking, he raised his hands and swept them upward in a small circle like a conductor, and we all came to our feet. After a short prayer, and maybe another hymn, he began to ask Mary and Jason a series of questions.

"Do you accept the gospel of God's grace in Jesus Christ revealed in the Holy Scriptures of the Old and New Testaments as the only way to eternal life?"

"I do," they answered.

"Do you acknowledge that you are a sinner, sinful by nature, but that by the grace of God alone your sins have been forgiven and your old nature put to death, so that you may be brought to newness of life and set apart as a member of the Body of Christ?"

"I do."

This Q and A went on for a few more minutes, covering promises to pray, seek God's guidance, grow in faith, attend church, and accept and obey the rules and guidance of the church elders. They responded with dutiful "I dos" and "I wills" at the end of each question.

Next, the members of the congregation were asked if they would welcome the woman and her son into the "community of faith" and if they would "pledge to them your love, your prayers, and your encouragement as they live the Christian life with us." The responses of the few dozen congregants in the large room sounded a little empty, as they delivered the best "We dos" and "We wills" they could muster. Not wanting to appear rude, I lip-synched the words along with the crowd.

Oh well, I thought, *I guess I could never become a member of this church.*

My understanding of the church-membership thing was still a little sketchy. Best I could tell, signing up with a certain church presupposed a heightened level of commitment, or maybe it just indicated that you intend to stick around. While I was okay with getting involved in some church activities or playing in the band, saying "I do" to anything involving Jesus was a commitment I was not willing, able, or interested in making.

Sure, given the havoc

> *"Saying 'I do' to anything involving Jesus was a commitment I was not willing, able, or interested in making."*

I had wrought on myself and on others in my twenties, I could almost accept the notion that I might be sinful by nature. I'd even come to a place in my thirties, through the literature and guidance of a 12-step program, where I could pray to a "power greater than myself" with some assurance that it was better to pray than not to pray. But Jesus? The Old and New Testaments? Eternal life? Martin believed in all of that stuff, but not me. Not today. Not tomorrow. No way.

I was hoping that the church-membership thing wouldn't extend the service longer than the usual one hour. I was pretty hungry and looking forward to endulging in some pancakes and syrup, even though yogurt and fruit would have been the more responsible option. As the announcements finished, Pastor Thomas began his sermon. The message was from the last book of the Bible, called Revelation.

The end of the world as we know it, oh my.

I knew very little about the Bible beyond my absolute confidence that, despite the heartfelt claims of the radio Christians, it was *not* the divinely inspired Word of God. I mean, how could it be? All of those writers with their hands all over it across the centuries and not one typo? I couldn't understand who in their right mind would ever believe that all of those angry monks and sadistic inquisitors never changed a little bit of this or that to tip the scales in their favor. How gullible could people be?

While it might have been a lovely notion that some benevolent creator of the universe whispered down two thousand pages of frequently contradictory text because he loves people, I believed the whole Christianity thing had started as an elaborate ruse, perpetrated by powerful and wealthy people to control the uneducated masses. Then, like some centuries-old version of the kids' game Telephone, the rules and the false hope they promised became a sad and pathetic crutch for the weak and a powerful hammer for the pious.

"I believed the whole Christianity thing had started as an elaborate ruse, perpetrated by powerful and wealthy people to control the uneducated masses."

Pastor Thomas started talking about Jesus' returning to earth—for what would be the end of the world—at a time that no one could predict. Judgment day. Armageddon. You don't need to be a Christian to be familiar with these terms and the notions they conjure. I was half-listening and wondering what any of this could ever have to do with me when he began to read:

> Then I saw Heaven open wide—and oh! A white horse and its Rider. The Rider named Faithful and True, judges and makes war in pure righteousness. His eyes are a blaze of fire, on his head many crowns. He has a Name inscribed that's known only to himself. He is dressed in a robe soaked with blood, and he is addressed as "Word of God." The armies of Heaven, mounted on white horses and dressed in dazzling white linen, follow him. A sharp sword comes out of his mouth so he can subdue the nations, then rule them with a rod of iron. He treads the winepress of the raging wrath of God, the Sovereign-Strong. On his robe and thigh is written, KING OF KINGS, LORD OF LORDS.

Apparently, unlike the love-everybody-Gandhi Jesus, the come-back-at-the-end-of-the-world Jesus is a wild warrior who'll show up ready to rumble.

A sword in his mouth? I thought. *These people are nuts.*

That's when my chest started to hurt.

At first it was just a small hollowness right below my sternum, like the sensation you get from swallowing too much pool water. Then came a wave of nausea. And then another. Finally, I started to have trouble catching my breath. *Did I eat something bad?* I wondered to myself. I hadn't eaten breakfast yet, so maybe last night. *Maybe indigestion?* My watch read 10:45.

Just fifteen more minutes, I thought as I began to break into a cold sweat.

I contemplated leaving, but I was on the center side of a twelve-foot-long pew, which left me with two equally untenable choices: either I walk up the wide center aisle between row after row of intricately carved wooden pews while clutching my chest and gasping for breath, or I climb over Martin, the kids, and another family to get to the side aisle to do the same. I looked left and then right, considering my options, and decided that both involved more drama than I was willing to risk. And I was just image conscious enough to risk death by heart attack to avoid it. So I drew another deep breath and tried to focus on keeping myself from throwing up.

"I was just image conscious enough to risk death by heart attack to avoid it. So I drew another deep breath and tried to focus on keeping myself from throwing up."

Martin, who was sitting to my right, was completely unaware of what I was going through. The heaviness of his eyelids, the rhythmic bobbing of his head, and his occasional half snore revealed that he was fighting a battle of his own. He could usually count on me for a gentle but firm elbow to the ribs when he was about to descend into REM sleep during a sermon, but today was different. As the minutes passed and my condition worsened, I had to admit that something was very, very wrong.

"Martin," I finally whispered with an uncharacteristic sense of urgency, "Baby, wake up."

"What?" he said, looking around. "I'm not sleeping."

"You're not going to believe this," I replied, ignoring his I'm-not-sleeping delusion, "but I think I might be having a freaking heart attack."

Martin had been with me long enough to know that I was more prone to ignore illness than to overstate it. Looking at me with a combination of uncertainty and concern, he asked, "Do you want to go to the hospital?"

"No," I said, still allowing self-consciousness to trump my mounting alarm. "Let's wait and see what happens."

Intent on maintaining my composure, I quietly struggled to catch a healthy breath and endure the distinct sensation that there was a five-hundred-pound weight perched squarely on the center of my chest.

Just five more minutes.

When the service ended, I took Martin's arm, and with the kids in tow, we made our way down the center aisle toward the exit. Trying to remain ever so dignified in the midst of my increasing distress, we weaved in and out of small groups of people as quickly as possible, intending to beat the exit traffic without drawing undue attention to ourselves. The church folks were in no hurry as they waited in line to be greeted by Pastor Thomas, who stood between us and the door.

Please don't try to talk to us. I have to get out of here.

Thankfully, an ancient woman whose curved body stood about four feet high had cornered Pastor Thomas, serving as a welcomed detour on the highway of people squeezing past them to make their way into the parking lot. Still holding on to Martin's arm to maintain my balance, I scurried to the car, fighting the sensation that my legs might go out from under me at any moment. *Come on, come on,* I repeated to myself. I needed to get into the car. I needed to get home. I needed . . . I needed . . . I didn't know what I needed, but I knew I *didn't* need to be standing in that parking lot.

Martin unlocked the passenger-side door and helped me lift myself into the seat of the SUV as he closed the door. The kids stuffed themselves into the backseat, ignorant of what I was going through and likely expecting me to ask where they'd like to go for brunch. But what they got was something very different.

The minute I found myself in the privacy of the car, a wave of intense emotion came over me. It was like a dam had broken, a flood of pent-up pressure released behind it in the form of sobbing and hysterical crying. Somewhere in the midst of all this, the pain in my chest lifted and there I was—generally a model of rigid self-control and modern accomplishment—crying ugly and repeating over and over again, "It is all true, all of it, it is all true." In that moment I knew I was not having a

> *"Somewhere in the midst of all this, the pain in my chest lifted, and there I was . . . crying ugly and repeating over and over again, 'It is all true, all of it, it is all true.'"*

heart attack. Instead, despite lifelong skepticism and outright animosity toward traditional religion, without asking or seeking, this skeptical atheist turned churchgoing agnostic had somehow been struck Christian.

CHAPTER TWO

Flirting with Faith

Looking back, I can now see that I'd actually spent a lifetime flirting with faith. There was something about religion and spirituality that attracted me on a primal level. Faith was my fantasy suitor. An unattainable ideal. Like a handsome stranger sitting across a crowded room or an iconic lead singer whose attention I could never hope to win, faith was an enticing unknown about which I often wondered, sometimes even fantasized, but never wholeheartedly pursued. Instead, I was the timid secret admirer, hidden behind a wall of bravado and self-sufficiency, undoubtedly unworthy of faith's attention.

In my teens and twenties I had given faith a shot. I read about it, talked about it, even tried to hook up a time or two, with less than stellar results. This lack of success only confirmed my suspicions. As appealing as it sometimes appeared, I became convinced that faith and I would never connect. Scorned in my would-be affections, I protected myself from further rejection by turning my attention to other pursuits. Eventually, I was able to convince myself that I had never really been attracted to faith in the first place. Yet, without my knowledge, faith had noticed me. I would soon learn that this seemingly unattainable suitor had intentions for me beyond anything I could imagine.

I don't recall hearing much about God at home when I was a kid, at least not in the traditional sense. When the question of religion did come up, it always seemed to be in the past tense—through reminisces both good and bad about what it was like for my parents to attend New York City Catholic schools in the 1950s and '60s or my brothers to attend them in grade school in the 1970s.

My parents were born and raised less than two blocks apart in the Marine Park section of Brooklyn, which I was taught to believe was the best borough in the City of New York. They shared similar childhood stories about the neighborhood: hanging out at the park or playing street games. Yet, when it came to their experiences with their Catholic educations, their stories were poles apart.

My mom loved church. During high school, she not only attended mass three times a day of her own volition but she took two trains and a bus (or was it two buses and a train?) to attend a special school for girls who felt called to become nuns. I recently came across a fantastic black-and-white picture of her at age sixteen, standing next to a much older nun. The two of them are looking directly into the camera and smiling, their faces small in the sea of white cloth that covered their heads and bodies as part of the habits donned by Dominican nuns in New York in the 1950s. When I asked my mom about the photo as an adult, she told me that her intent had been to be a missionary. She planned to join the Dominicans first and then become affiliated with the Maryknoll order to do mission work.

My father's Catholic-school stories conjured less peaceful images. He remembered enduring corporal punishment at the hands of strict nuns and the Christian brothers—rulers to the knuckles, paddles to the bottom, and the occasional punch in the face. The images of my dad's nuns were hard, angry, and bordering on sadistic, offering a stark contrast to those smiling faces in white contained in that old three-by-three-inch photograph of my mother.

The same batch of old pictures depict my father with turned-up jeans over white socks and loafers or motorcycle boots and a white T-shirt with a pack of cigarettes rolled in the sleeve. His blond hair was slicked back and set off his light blue eyes, which were striking enough to be remarkable even in black-and-white photos. My mom's style equally captured the late fifties ideal, replete with fitted pencil skirts, tailored sweaters, bobby socks, and perfectly polished saddle shoes.

As I recall the story, my father would park himself on one of the red leather-covered stools at the counter of the corner luncheonette and watch for my mother to walk down the block from the three-bedroom attached house that she shared with her parents and six siblings. "I'm going to marry that girl," he'd say to himself, long before she chose having a family over becoming a nun. Fortunately for me, my three brothers, and my sister, my father was right.

Despite his attendance at Catholic schools, my father was no choirboy. In fact, my mother laughed so hard she cried when she told me about one of their first dates, after he returned from his tour of Army duty in Europe as part of the post–Korean War draft. They'd dated a few times before he left, but didn't really keep in touch while he was gone. Upon his return, he reconnected with my mother *and* an old girlfriend from the neighborhood. When my mother caught wind of the other girl, my dad had to make a choice. His decision was obvious, but it didn't come cheap. On their very next date, my mother hauled him into confession at St. Patrick's Cathedral so they could start their relationship off right. Now that my father was duly forgiven by God (and my mother), they patched things up and were married less than a year later, in November of 1960.

> *"Despite his attendance in Catholic schools, my father was no choirboy."*

By 1971, with five kids under the age of ten, my parents decided that the time was right to get out of the city and move "upstate." We were part of a large wave of middle-class families who migrated in the late 1960s and early 1970s from the outlying boroughs of New York to rural towns within an hour's drive of the city. Most of the men were firemen, like my father, or policemen and other city workers—hundreds of young families leaving the city in search of cheap real estate and safe public schools.

We ended up in a small farm town called Warwick that wouldn't transition from rural to suburban until the 1990s. In what seemed like an instant, we went from living on a close-knit city block in Brooklyn to a house perched on the side of a mountain that was too steep for the school bus to climb. Between trips to the grocery store, we walked to the local dairy farm, where we bought our milk straight from the farmer in a silver milk can and purchased eggs, sometimes still warm, from a small local egg farm. Even at age six, I experienced culture shock.

My mother, who was home with us full time, embraced the rural lifestyle. She enrolled my brothers and me in 4-H, a nationwide farm organization where we learned about crafts and cooking, did community-service projects, and entered our wares in the county fair. As if that weren't enough, by age ten I became an avid cattle judger, an odd experience that I've used with surprising success when answering the standard interview query, "Where did you get started in communications?" posed by more than one New York City hiring manager.

This city-to-country transition was not the only shift during those early years as my parents built our family. Somewhere between my birth in 1966 and the time we moved upstate, my parents stopped going to church. It must have happened gradually, since we were all baptized, but only my two older brothers had their first Holy Communions and attended Catholic school. This left me, as the middle child, on the spiritual cusp.

––––––

Six years old and new to "the country," I recall three things that I wanted to define me. I was Irish, I was Catholic, and I was from Brooklyn. Unfortunately, none of these identifiers was actually true. First, my family had been in the United States for generations, and my adopted Irish heritage was just part of my German, Scotch, and ultimately melting-pot American background. Next, while I embraced this notion of being Catholic and was surrounded by people who had been raised in the Catholic faith, I was not part of that community and had little understanding of what it meant. And finally, now that we had moved to Warwick, I was no longer a city girl, although I did my best to pretend that I was.

As I got a little older and approached the age when I had lived almost as many years in "the country" as I had in "the city," the seed of divergence between the person I wanted to be and the person I really was began to germinate. It seemed critically important in my ten-year-old mind to retain my city-girl image. And so I learned to bury my highly sensitive nature in a variety of creative and self-destructive ways. This façade extended to school, where the influx of families who had moved from New York to this rural farm town had created a Hatfields versus McCoys division between the new kids and the local kids. In my estimation, you were either from the city (cool) or not (a hick). Being both and neither—a vantage point I now tend to find myself in frequently—I thought the best way to keep my fourth-grade city-girl street cred intact was to claim to have gone to Catholic school.

All the *real* city people seemed to have gone to Catholic school. And applying elementary-school logic, the Brooklyn identity rested in the Catholic identity, and the Catholic identity rested, not in participation in the faith, but in participation in Catholic education. My mother had done it; my father had done it. My aunts and uncles and brothers had done it. Most of the new kids moving up from the city and coming to school with me had done it. This, I reasoned, was a critical rite

> *"Six years old and new to 'the country,' I recall three things that I wanted to define me. . . . Unfortunately, none of these identifiers was actually true."*

of passage, and I needed to get in on it. I could care less about the God part—I just wanted to fit in.

"You didn't go to Catholic school," two recent transplants from Staten Island taunted me.

"Yeah, I did." I replied, hand on my little hip, trying to retrieve as much of my rapidly disappearing Brooklyn accent as I could muster.

"Oh, yeah, where?"

My brothers had gone to St. Thomas Aquinas elementary school on Hendrickson Street in Brooklyn. That lie would have been a sure bet, but for some reason I decided to get creative.

"P.S. 222," I said with complete confidence.

They looked at each other and started to laugh.

"P.S. 222, are you kidding?"

I wasn't kidding. But I began to get an uneasy feeling. They knew something I didn't. I did go to P.S. 222 for kindergarten in Brooklyn, and I knew it wasn't a Catholic school. But these guys were all the way from Staten Island— how could they possibly know that?

"No, I am not kidding. What is your problem?" I couldn't understand why they didn't believe me. It was like having a hole in your pants or a "kick me" sign on your back. I knew I was exposed, but was unsure where and how.

They were laughing harder now, and I was starting to get upset.

"P.S. 222 stands for Public School 222, you idiot. Everyone knows that."

My heart sank. The only thing worse than getting caught red-handed in a lie is getting caught in one that knocks a feigned identity out from under you. In one fell swoop I was outed on two fronts. Not only did I not know the most basic info about my Brooklyn-girl façade, I didn't even know enough about the ins and outs of Catholic school to lie about it. I had blown it.

I learned an unfortunate lesson that day that would fuel my interaction with people, consciously and unconsciously, for years to come: if you are going to create a false persona, your backstory needs to be airtight. I spent the next thirty years perfecting the art of maintaining one image or another, and trying to feel comfortable in my own skin. You never would have known this if you'd met me, though. My inner chameleon remained well masked under a veneer of bravado that thickened like a deep, textured scar over the real me until not even I knew what was underneath. I was like a living, breathing paper doll, cutting out little outfits, accessories, and facial expressions to meet the needs of whatever situation I found myself in.

Of course, I did not know it at the time.

Instead, I took on new images and personas—from people-pleasing teen, to avant-garde bohemian in my twenties, to buttoned-up executive in my thirties—believing each time that *this* must be my genuine self. What choice did I have? There was nothing beneath the surface to grab onto. I seemed to come into focus only when I was wearing something, accomplishing something, or saying something that

> *"If you are going to create a false persona, your backstory needs to be airtight."*

fulfilled one of my trumped-up identities. Might it have been different if I'd been brought up within a faith tradition? Maybe. Then again, I've met way too many churchgoers who struggle with similar identity issues to prescribe that simple a cure for such a complex malady.

———

I never quite pieced together the reason that my parents cut their ties with the Catholic church. I recall asking my mother once when I was a kid and her saying something about the contradiction between the opulence of the Vatican and the plight of the poor, but I never really got a clear answer. Maybe there wasn't a clear answer. Maybe there was, and it was none of my business. Years later when I asked her again, she said she wasn't entirely sure why they had stopped. She'd wondered, she also told me, if we kids might have benefited from growing up with some conception of God and faith. And yet, she told me, "I always thought you would find your own way."

Little did I know, my way would find me.

A Note to Skeptics

This might be a good time to take a moment to directly address those of you who think I am making all of this up. I know you're out there. Those of you who, even if you believe in the existence of God and Jesus and the Holy Spirit, don't believe that he, she, or it would have the time or the inclination to drop in on suburban New York to knock some PR executive for a loop and transform her life by shaking it up beyond recognition. I'm talking to those of you in the "She probably had a panic attack" contingent or the "So you're telling me that you went to church one day and magically became Christian; how very nice for you" folks. I'm stepping out of the story to reach out to you for one simple reason.

I am you.

Six years ago, there was no way I would have believed this story. In fact, I'm still enough of a skeptic that I question most of what I encounter in this faith. I can understand your thinking that a supernatural transformation resulting from a brush with God is ridiculous. It is the stuff bad movies and institutionalizations are made of.

"*This unlikely encounter with the Divine relieved me of the luxury of unbelief.*"

I couldn't agree more.

What happened to me is entirely unbelievable. In fact, there have been many times since my experience that I thought I might wake to find that I'd dreamed the whole thing, or that I'd come to and discover I'd had a nervous breakdown or a bad acid trip. And yet, despite my own best thinking on the matter—and the fact that I am (mostly) mentally competent and decades away from my last experience with psychedelics—I am left with a simple truth: the Joan I was and the Joan I am are undeniably two very different women. Somehow, without an emotional altar call, or threats of hellfire and brimstone, or the softening that comes from the pain of a personal tragedy, this unlikely encounter with the Divine relieved me of the luxury of unbelief.

Without asking or praying or doing anything to encourage it, I was infused with this . . . *something*. I didn't have words for it then, and after six years of dedicating myself to pursuing it, I still don't. Since that experience at church, I've spent many days and nights trying to define it, capture it, and put it in a box. But the more I learn, the more I see that static definitions of this encounter fall short.

So my question has become, How exactly do I even begin to describe receiving God's grace in such a dramatic and bizarre way, especially since, at the time, I had absolutely no context for what that really meant? Moreover, how could I conceive that this singular experience was more a beginning than an end? It was like the first stitch in an elaborate tapestry that would continue to weave itself into an unknown pattern for the rest of my life. I could not have known that this con-version of heart was the threshold through which I would walk into a dramatic, sometimes painful, thoroughly reorient-ing and always exciting change of life. Now that I'm getting it all down on paper, I realize that it might read like fiction or, even worse, fantasy. And yet, I cannot deny that I have come to believe deeply enough to actually follow this faith and allow it to transform every aspect of my life—inside and out. I'd say that I had no choice, but of course I did. The same kind of choice as you have when you are drowning and some-one throws you a life jacket.

But I wasn't drowning.

In fact, on that morning in 2003, I was happier than I had ever been in my life. Far from the I-have-everything-I-ever-wanted-but-feel-like-something-is-missing circumstance that plagues some people when they approach their forties, I was content. As far as I was concerned, my life was perfect. I was the last person who needed some come-to-Jesus moment.

Having spent the years on either side of Y2K living the you-can-do-anything-you-put-your-mind-to message of my childhood, I'd pulled myself up by my bootstraps after a few false starts and gone from living hand to mouth as a single mother with two children in my late twenties to being a suc-cessful PR executive ten years later. In the process of turning my life around, I'd learned to skillfully juggle the demands of a healthy, happy family and a satisfying career—all while pur-suing the American dream. Our rambling four-thousand-square-foot home was filled with beautiful furnishings, stylish clothing, and all of the latest goods and gadgets for making life more comfortable and entertaining. When we found the time (which wasn't often) and the energy (which was usually expended), Martin, the kids, and I enjoyed the company of our extended family and close friends, and we found interesting ways to spend our considerable disposable income.

Sure, keeping all of those balls in the air wasn't always easy. And there were times when Martin and I reminisced about our dating days, when he'd taught me to play guitar and the two of us would sing and play music together. But once we got married, we never once considered that grasping for the brass ring was anything but the right thing to do. When my life's pendulum had swung from bedlam to accomplishment in the mid-1990s, any notion of living the offbeat bohemian lifestyle I thought I had wanted in my twenties was traded for predictability and order—my best version of it, anyway.

This meant becoming an intense, multitasking control freak, which I viewed as a necessary evil for a have-it-all woman with my full and hectic lifestyle. Sunday nights were spent updating a half-dozen to-do lists for the week. There was one for work, another for Martin and the kids, one for household business, one for managing real estate and other investments, and one for personal needs like doctor's appointments, oil changes, and manicures. I'd hit the ground running on Monday mornings: out of bed, to the gym, at my home-office desk by 8:30, recovery meeting at lunch, back to my desk by 1:30, after-school activities, home office for a little more work, order dinner (I rarely cooked), then even more work or an evening activity of some sort. By 8:00 or 9:00 P.M., I'd collapse on the couch with Martin for a few hours of mindless TV until we'd fall asleep and drag ourselves

"Why would I take on the burden of religion when doing it myself was working out just fine?"

upstairs at 2:00 A.M., only to wake up at 6:00 A.M. and do it all over again.

All I had to do was look around at our house, our cars, our clothes, and the other fruits of our labor to see that the tight schedule was worth it. I loved this lifestyle. I felt none of the guilt, emptiness, or longing for something deeper or more meaningful that many people describe when they "arrive." Nope. Life was good, and I was utterly content.

That's why this Christian thing made absolutely no sense.

Why would I take on the burden of religion when doing it myself was working out just fine? I didn't know the answer to that question, but I had to admit that, while I might have preferred *any* other explanation, something spiritual or religious had indeed happened to me. When the dust finally settled in the days following that June morning and things didn't go back to "normal," I had to admit to myself the disconcerting truth. I hadn't had a heart attack. I'd experienced a profound and transformational change of heart.

My Way

Finding my way to faith, as my mother had predicted I would, involved times of seeking and times of abandoning the search in exchange for the certainty of unbelief. Like many kids in or outside of church circles, I spent my college years searching for something—maybe anything—to believe in.

Anything but Jesus, that is.

I left Warwick in 1984 with great fanfare. Eighteen years old and full of promise, I was a varsity athlete, class president, prom queen, and honor student; and I was off to study engineering at the U.S. Air Force Academy. Early acceptance to USAFA through a primary congressional nomination was an honor and an accomplishment, although for me it was more of a relief. Our family of seven fell into a financial-aid no-man's-land: my father made too much for us to qualify for assistance and not enough to help with tuition. This left me far more interested in the prestigious (and free) education that the academy afforded than I was in pursuing a career in the military.

My year in Colorado Springs as a plebe cadet (short for "plebian," the lowest commoners in ancient Rome) at the Air Force Academy taught me two important things. First, I discovered in myself an abhorrence for the hypocrisy of an organization that required me to respect rank over substance. I could endure the most intense hazing (which they called "training" because hazing was not allowed) from impeccably turned-out cadets with shined shoes and belt buckles so clean that you could do your makeup in them. It was clear that they believed in what they were doing enough to carry it out personally. But I was repulsed by people who did not live what they were training—like the overweight cadet with the wrinkled shirt and scuffed shoes who would train a plebe cadet, male or female, to the point of tears and walk away laughing.

I knew midway through my freshman year that the air force was not for me; however, I decided to stick it out until June so I could know that I had *transferred* rather than quit. This was a distinction that made little difference to anyone but me—and maybe my father, who had hoped I might change my mind.

Which leads to a second lesson that began to surface during that year in Colorado: I was an arrogant, self-centered, know-it-all whose actions and attitudes were every bit as hypocritical as the people whose hypocrisy I loathed. I just didn't realize it yet.

Glimpses of my character defects surfaced intermittently in the form of broken rules and a questionable attitude. I would pound them down like the gophers that pop up in those arcade games, where the player hits them on the head with a foam-covered mallet. Inevitably, Pride would peek out from beneath the surface and feed the warm feeling I would get when one of my rivals (or even my friends) was upbraided a moment after I was praised. Then sister Ego would surface, fueling the self-affirming pleasure I felt when my trim roommate gained a few pounds at the same time I'd lost a few. Of

"These rogue thoughts were my dirty little secrets, hidden from view until a field-training exercise exposed them—and me."

course, these rogue thoughts were my dirty little secrets, hidden from view until a field-training exercise exposed them—and me.

A team of four or five of us had been given a limited time (minutes, not hours) to run through a series of physical barriers: high walls, wide pools of water, and other challenges that were impossible to navigate alone but doable if we worked as a team. We took turns leading and following, and were observed by upperclassmen who critiqued our performance. I can't recall my behavior as a follower, but when it was time for me to lead, propelled by my competitive and people-pleasing nature, I was ready to show them what I was made of.

"Set . . . go!" A shrill whistle sounded, and my team moved forward to the base of a ten-foot-high, perfectly smooth wall. We had to develop and execute a strategy to get each member of our team over it to even see the next challenge.

"Maybe you can boost me up on top," a fellow cadet suggested to another team member, throwing out the first idea to get us started.

"Definitely . . ." the second cadet responded. "I could . . ."

"Wait a second," I interrupted, whining. Yup. Standing there in full fatigues with an unloaded weapon in my hand, I whined like a child. "I am the leader in this exercise." What I really meant was that, as the leader, I planned to have the ideas and tell my team what to do. That was what my friends Pride and Ego had taught me about working with others, and as an apt pupil I did not intend to disappoint. So my team and I spent the duration of the training exercise arguing about who should be making the decisions and how we should work together, rather than addressing the task at hand.

"Burger." An upper-class cadet whose stellar leadership of our unit had earned my respect shouted my maiden name as he blew the whistle a second time to signify that our time was up. "This mission was a complete failure."

You're right it was a complete failure, I thought. *If only my team had listened to me, we would have nailed it.* Standing at attention, I shouted back one of the four responses—yes, sir; no, sir; no excuse, sir; or sir, may I ask a question—that a plebe cadet was allowed when faced with a question (or attack) from an upperclassman. "Yes, sir."

"And you were the cause."

What? Having learned the hard way that there was no sense trying to argue with an angry senior cadet, I responded, "Yes, sir." He went on to call me out on the whining and the fighting and the poor example of facilitation that my need to be right and give orders had illustrated. *How could this be my fault?* I was confused and embarrassed. The looks on the faces of my fellow cadets made it clear that he was accurate in his assessment, but I was still in the dark about why. Pride and Ego giggled, having won another round without my having detected them.

When I had left for Colorado a year earlier, I had never once considered that I might leave the academy. As far as I was concerned, the nine years from age eighteen to twenty-seven would be prescribed by Uncle Sam and his friends in Colorado Springs, so I had no Plan B. I arrived home in June 1985 unsure of who I was, what I was about, or what I should do next.

> *"Having spent most of my salary on booze and drugs, I arrived in Albany carrying little more than a gargantuan chip on my shoulder."*

Facing an uncertain future, I spent that summer living in Brooklyn with my older brother, waiting tables on the night shift at the Floridian Diner on Flatbush Avenue and selling the *New York Post* to drivers crossing from Brooklyn to Staten Island on the Verrazano Bridge. This transition from highly structured military life to complete freedom set me off like a spinning top. Having spent most of my salary on booze and drugs, I arrived in Albany carrying little more than a gargantuan chip on my shoulder. My commitment to high achievement and people pleasing had not disappeared; it was just folded into a stew of self-pity and rage, laying the groundwork for what would become a completely bifurcated life. Juggling both a hearty appetite for drugs, alcohol, and dangerous behavior and an intense desire to succeed, I put myself through college, earned a BA in economics, and became a licensed stockbroker by the time I was twenty.

It was during these years in Albany that I, for the first time since grade school, became interested in faith. I can't recall when it started, but I am sure it had something to do with my roommate, Darcy. I answered an ad for a single room in a four-bedroom apartment and walked in the front door on my first visit to find a three-foot-tall bong and a bag of pot on the coffee table.

Ahh, I thought. *Home, sweet, home.*

I said yes on the spot, left a cash deposit, and moved my things—which fit on the front passenger seat of my car—into the space the next day.

Darcy and I hit it off quickly, which was surprising since she was about as different from a recently discharged Air Force Academy cadet on an anger-induced bender as one could be. She was a free spirit with piles of untamed curls on her head and a generous smile, from which erupted a hearty belly laugh at the slightest hint of levity. She rarely wore shoes or a bra, or a care in the world—the perfect yin to my twelve-months-of-eating-meals-at-attention yang. An aspiring artist and musician who liked to drink and get high as much as I did, she helped me embrace the creative side of myself, which had been hidden under layers of high expectations and aspirations for success.

When we weren't in class or tending bar or wait-ressing, the two of us spent long hours in jazz cafes and

> "When I walked in the front door, I saw a three-foot-tall bong and a bag of pot on the coffee table and thought, Ahh. Home, sweet, home."

bars—Darcy sketching un-
suspecting patrons, and me
writing stories about them
in bound journals. We
browsed used-book stores
and traded records (actual
vinyl records) at a small
used-record exchange. We
also frequented a New Age

"One book, one crystal, and one tab of acid at a time, I sought to find some transcendent truth."

store that hosted meditation and jewelry-making classes,
which turned me on to all kinds of spiritual practices that I
had never known about or considered. It was in this quagmire
of post-academy uncertainty and new experiences that I
began to explore the supernatural and spirituality. Like so
many other things I had done before and since, I fell into this
quest with little intention.

One book, one crystal, and one tab of acid at a time, I
sought to find some transcendent truth. Looking back on
it, I think I may have been looking for something to
ground me. Having derived my sense of good and bad,
right and wrong, from the outside in, I was living like a
driver on a backcountry road in the middle of the night. I
knew the law said drive fifty-five, but, hey, if nobody's
looking I can drive as far and as fast as I want. And I was
speeding out of control.

I explored the notions that cosmic energy could flow
through crystals and that I might find guidance by throwing
the I Ching. I read the Bhagavad Gita and studied *The
Teachings of the Compassionate Buddha*. Once, I even picked
up a copy of the Satanic Bible at my favorite used-book store,
figuring that the authentic seeker does not discriminate. I

read the first chapter one night before bed, then woke up around 3:00 A.M. riddled with free-floating fear and a distinct sense that the book was the culprit, so I threw on a coat and kicked the book to the curb—literally and figuratively. In retrospect, this was probably my first genuine, albeit creepy, spiritual experience.

All in all, religion and spiritual practices began to fascinate me, and I had a desire to claim something of my own. Yet the apparent contradictions and lack of rationality I came across in my ragtag study fried my logical brain. I wish I could recall a specific moment in time when I shifted from searching for faith to deciding that there was nothing there for me, but this spirit of self-reliance crept in over time. Ayn Rand's books *Atlas Shrugged* and *The Fountainhead* had a profound impact on my worldview in those years. Her characters' worship of intellect, science, and dedication to hard work dovetailed with my growing sense that, despite my desire and willingness to search for faith, there was nothing out there to find. This evolving atheism, coupled with a growing reliance on drugs and alcohol as guide and comforter, just seemed to fit me better. It was easier. I could make sense of it. If there was nothing up or out there, and if I had a mechanism to escape when I needed to, what else did I need? I found my religion by abandoning religion. Now I could get on with the business of mastering my own destiny.

> *"This evolving atheism, coupled with a growing reliance on drugs and alcohol as guide and comforter, just seemed to fit me better."*

It didn't take long for me to learn that I am not very good at destiny mastering. After graduating from college at the age of twenty, I landed a job as a stockbroker trainee in Albany. My coworkers had no idea that this young up-and-comer was balancing days in the office with harrowing nights that often ended within an hour or two of the next work day. Surrounded by people with a similar lifestyle, I found it easy to believe that this balancing act was not only desirable but also that it was, somehow, normal. Of course, living this kind of lie works only until the bottom falls out.

My rapid decline from broker to broken began with the stock market crash of 1987 and gained speed through a short stint as a traveling salesperson for a Fortune 500 company, a working trip through Europe, and a whirlwind of unfortunate decisions that could fill a book of their own. By 1992, an ill-fated three-year marriage to the father of my two older children had run its course.

Despite what had appeared outwardly to be an excellent start, I found myself back in Warwick in my late twenties: a single mother with two beautiful children, waiting tables to make ends meet and racking my brain to figure out how I'd squandered what seemed to be an incredibly bright future. My rationalization was to add the market crash and my ex-husband to a growing list of hard-luck frustrations that explained why a person with my smarts and skills was not living the successful life I'd been born to live. Focused on the immediate survival of myself and my kids, I had little time, energy, or inclination to indulge in honest self-reflection.

The early 1990s were difficult, humbling days, and a time of my life that is difficult to write about for many reasons, including the fact that I don't remember it very well. The human brain has a way of protecting itself from painful memories, and mine works overtime when it comes to those years when it was Andrew, Kelsey, and me against the world. In many ways, the kids remember more of it than I do, and the stories—which even they will admit are sometimes exaggerated for dramatic effect—involve their mother walking around like a zombie much of the time, emotionally unavailable and utterly exhausted.

"The kids' memories involve their mother walking around like a zombie much of the time, emotionally unavailable and utterly exhausted."

Thankfully, I kept my drinking and drugging antics, which had settled down considerably compared to my college days but were still going strong, to myself. I got a babysitter and went out with friends to a local bar on occasion, but mostly I'd just roll a joint, pour myself a drink, and allow myself to zone out in front of the television in the evenings, after the kids were tucked in their beds. My wildest days were behind me. Now I was just numb.

Meanwhile, in a twist of spiritual fate, I had enrolled Andrew and Kelsey in a preschool at a local Baptist church that met my scheduling and budget needs better than other schools I might have chosen. There I was, trying to dig myself

out from under, devoid of faith and sure that if there was a
God (which there wasn't), he wouldn't allow people like me
to struggle so much. At the same time, my kids were learning
Bible stories and singing songs about Jesus.

Spiritual irony at its finest.

He Said, She Said

It was during those postdivorce years in the mid-1990s that I first started spending time with Martin. I had met him four or five years earlier, when he was dating a friend of mine. In another ironic twist, he and my friend used to occasionally babysit for Andrew and Kelsey when the kids were still in diapers. Back then, despite my own questionable circumstances, I was still way too much of an image-conscious snob to ever consider dating him. While fun-loving and kind, Martin was a construction worker from South America with a GED. Sure, I was down on my luck, but not *that* down on my luck. Even after my first marriage ended and he and my friend broke up, I never once thought about a romantic relationship with him. He was just a friend.

But it wasn't just Martin. The thought of getting involved in a relationship with *anybody* was beyond my comprehension. I dated one man for a very brief time after the divorce, which confirmed my suspicion that I had way too much baggage to make a healthy choice when it came to a relationship. And I was tired. To be frank, my twenties had taken a toll on me, and the blade on my knife of intuition was dull. With my time at the academy, the blur that was my time in Albany, the whirlwind that was my first marriage, and my return to Warwick with my tail between my legs, I didn't know which end was up. I had no idea who I was, so how could I begin to know what kind of man might be right for me and my kids?

So I went on the wagon with respect to men (I'd not yet hit the drug and alcohol wagon) and tried to keep the focus on what was important: making a living and taking care of my children.

As the weeks and months passed, Martin and I began to hang out more frequently. Relegated to the late evenings after the kids were in bed—since I did not want to be one of those women whose kids had a host of Uncle Bobs and Uncle Jacks hanging around the house—he would sometimes fix a leaky sink or do some other mundane task around the house before we'd watch a movie or stumble through Indigo Girls tunes on the guitar.

One night I noticed myself putting on some makeup before he came over and actually caring about what I put on. *I'm dressing up for him*, I thought, shaking my head as I blushed and giggled at myself in the mirror. He told me later that he had noticed the shift and was doing the same, but tried not to make it as obvious as I had. After all of these years and a less than stellar track record with men, I felt like a teenager again.

But I was not a teenager. I was an exhausted, worn-out, extremely tentative woman whom Martin jokingly began to call White Fang, because I was "beautiful like a wolf and just as deadly." I had been through the ringer, and no matter who or what was to blame, I was on guard. That thick armor of protection that I had begun to craft in my childhood transplant to the country had become a shield. Nobody would ever hurt me again; I would make sure of it. It was this Everest that Martin chose to climb, and after more than three months of nondating, our relationship shifted from friends to something more. Despite the odds, it was one of the first healthy decisions I had made in years.

———————

Andrew and Kelsey were about four and five at the time and had hit the relentless "why" stage.

"Why is the sky blue?"

"Why does it rain?"

And since they were attending a Christian preschool, "Why don't we go to church?"

I had some impressive scientific answers to the blue sky and rain questions, but the church thing was a little more complicated.

I was cool with being an atheist, but somehow it seemed better to arrive at rabid unbelief through trial and error, not through your mom. I had to figure out what to tell these kids. When I asked Martin his thoughts about church and religion, I was surprised by his response.

"I am a Christian," he told me without hesitation.

"A Christian?" I responded, wrinkling my nose like I had just smelled rotten fish. I'd known him for years, but had no idea. "But not like a *Christian* Christian, right?"

> *"I was cool with being an atheist, but somehow it seemed better to arrive at rabid unbelief through trial and error, not through your mom."*

Even I wasn't exactly sure what I meant by that. It just didn't seem that a guy who looked like Frank Zappa and dated a pot-smoking, booze-drinking, atheist single mother of two could be a real Christian. Add to that the fact that he played guitar and didn't expect more from me than I was able to give, and he became the most unusual specimen of a church person I had ever met. When we started discussing the kids' religious questions, he didn't preach or judge. He just believed and gave me space to not believe.

As the kids' questions became more frequent, Martin and I spent hours discussing God and faith at the tiny table in the kitchen of my apartment. As desperate as I was to debate the finer points of why it would be absolutely impossible for Noah's ark to hold two of every animal of every species, Martin refused to engage.

It's not that he was unsure about what he believed. In fact, his faith in Jesus and confidence in the truth of the Bible were disarmingly resolute. He just never tried to convert me to his way of thinking, nor did he belittle or attack my reliance on logic, rationality, and science to explain the world. Instead, he shared his convictions, listened to mine, and let go of the outcome.

I had a very different approach.

"So you are telling me with a straight face that you believe there was a guy named Adam. A real flesh-and-blood guy named Adam," I would ask, more disgusted than astonished.

"Uh-huh," he would reply with little interest, lighting a cigarette and taking a sip of coffee. He knew where this was going (nowhere), so he refused to invest himself in the tit for tat.

I would have preferred if he'd come back at me. I wanted him to defend himself. But he never did. He didn't need me to believe. All that freedom just made me push harder.

"But there is no way all of the people of the world of all races and nationalities came from one guy. What? Did he have multiracial DNA?" Some part of me must have known how absolutely stupid that sounded, but I couldn't help myself.

"I don't like to complicate it," he'd say to me in different ways, over and over again, referring to his faith in the truth of the Bible. "I can't explain it. I have no desire to explain it." The words were delivered in a loving, honest tone. He really believed, and he was gentle and nondogmatic about it. This confounded me. And for some reason, it really bothered me. I just couldn't let it go.

"That is a cop-out. You can't just *believe*."

In those days, debating religion with me was like running a marathon. Agreeing to disagree was not an option. I needed to prove that I was right. Rather than listening, I ruthlessly defended my position, even though some part of me must have found it lacking, since I was uncertain about teaching it to my kids.

Instead, I filled ashtrays and emptied coffeepots, trying to share my faith in the futility of faith. But I didn't just share these thoughts with Martin; I tried to impose them on him. I felt compelled to debunk his beliefs, convinced that my intellect could set him straight. While at the time I thought I was motivated by sharing my perception of the "truth," my primary interest was winning.

Martin listened patiently. He even admitted that the logistics of Noah and his ark were beyond his imagination. But to my utter amazement and ever-increasing annoyance, he was perfectly comfortable not having all of the answers. "If I could explain every part of it," he'd say, "then I wouldn't need faith."

The notion of having that kind of blind faith was beyond

> *"I didn't quite raise myself to the level of God. More like the Queen of the Universe."*

me. I needed proof. I applied logic. I could not imagine believing so strongly in something I could not see, hear, smell, touch, or taste. Sure, my life was a mess. I was drinking too much and working way below my potential, but I was sure of one thing: I was the only one who was going to get myself out of it. Not some God or some words in a book. I just needed to figure out my next move and get it together. I was confident that things were going to turn around and that *I* would make it happen. Perhaps I wasn't an atheist, after all. I believed in myself. I didn't quite raise myself to the level of God. More like the Queen of the Universe.

Little did I know that my reign was about to end.

CHAPTER SIX

By the Book

Can you believe I am a freaking born-again Christian?" I was shaking my head in disbelief as I finally admitted out loud to Martin what I'd been thinking and writing in my journal for days. A week or so had passed since I'd been "struck," and given my nonstop babbling about how I suddenly knew that my steps were being guided by God, I'm guessing he had already figured it out.

Martin's response was typical. He tended to take most things in stride, especially when it came to me and things involving God. When he and his family arrived in the United States, they attended the kind of church that encouraged and embraced the demonstration of the presence of the Holy Spirit in their congregants. As a result, he was used to a faith with lots of activity—hands in the air, speaking in tongues, dancing, and whooping it up to the glory of God. So, while he hadn't experienced God in quite the same way I had, the notion that a supernatural smack-down was possible was not outside the realm of his beliefs or his imagination. That said, he had learned to be skeptical of demonstrative manifestations of the faith—not because he did not believe that God could or would engage people in this way but because he thought that some people wanted it so badly they would go to any lengths to have it.

Martin's favorite example of this is of a woman who came to his church youth group to "teach" the kids how to speak in tongues. Martin was about sixteen at the time, and though he loved the youth group and has fond memories of it to this day, he spent most of his time sitting in the back making jokes with his friends. The youth leaders were young themselves, so they took it in stride. Not so for this woman, whom Martin jokingly refers to as "the tongues lady."

After explaining to the group of teens ranging in age from fourteen to eighteen that she intended to instruct them in the ways of speaking in tongues, she began, "Okay, now I would like all of you to repeat after me, hallelujah, hallelujah, halle-lujah, hallelujah."

Martin and his friends rolled their eyes as they muttered under their breath as the rest of the group, who were a little less cynical, followed the instructions.

"Hallelujah, hallelujah, hallelujah."

As they continued, she encouraged them, "Faster, faster!"

"Hallelujah, hallelujah, hallelujah."

When the syllables began to run together into a form of "lu, lu, lu, lu, lu" she pointed at them and, as if halting a game of musical chairs, shouted "tongues!"

Martin and his friends buried their faces in their hands, their heads on the tables in front of them, in a fruitless at-tempt to hide their laughter.

"Lu, lu, lu, lu," Martin mocked her under his breath.

"What is so funny?" the tongues lady asked, calling Martin to the front of the room . . .

Neither this glorified parlor trick nor the reprimand that followed was enough to convince Martin that a tongue twister and speaking in tongues were the same thing. Nor was it enough to make him question his faith. But it did leave him a little suspicious of those who claim to manifest demonstrations of the Holy Spirit on command.

And yet, Martin told me later, he saw that something was different when my conversion happened to me.

He had been with me when I was an avowed atheist, and he was sitting next to me in the pew for the spring morning conversion. Martin believed me, he said, precisely because what I had experienced was so unbelievable. Not only had I endured a rather charismatic (and uncomfortable) conversion, I had done so in about the least charismatic church one could imagine. No tongues lady. No altar call. These people didn't even clap at the end of a song. I had no idea at the time that coming to this faith in this way— without seeking, asking, or praying for it—made me something of a spiritual oddball. Sure, it seemed weird, but the Christianity thing had always seemed weird to me, so this was just par for the course. I'd heard the term "born again" and pooh-poohed it with little thought about what it really meant. But now I found myself knee deep in faith, trying to figure out exactly what to do with it.

"Martin believed me, he said, precisely because what I had experienced was so unbelievable."

Try to put yourself in my shoes. You've spent the better part of your life mocking and challenging the notion of God—specifically the Judeo-Christian God and all that goes with it. Far from understanding God as some kind of merciful redeemer, or gradually growing into an understanding of who he is and what he wants for you, you are suddenly hit with the full power and scope of an indescribable force or influence or something. I'm not sure how you'd feel, but I was like, *Where do I $#@& start?*

I spent three weeks talking about God to anyone who would listen and writing dozens of pages a day in journals before the thought occurred to me: *The Bible! You should read the Bible.*

I know, I know. This is not rocket science. But the morning this thought came to me, it was clear that this was more than just a good idea. "Somehow I know that the answers to what I am supposed to do next are somewhere in that book," I wrote in a journal entry. But *where* in that book?

I couldn't imagine picking up a two-thousand-plus page tome and reading it cover to cover, hoping to get a little direction about what to do next. Having come to the faith table a little too late in the game to start off on the wrong track, I felt as if I'd walked out into the middle of a frozen lake and heard a giant, heart-stopping *craaaak* underneath my feet. I didn't want to take a single step until I knew my compass was pointing north.

Unsure where to begin, I figured I might as well go straight to the day-to-day. *I'm a wife and a mother*, I thought. *Let me see what this book has to say about that.* I went to the index in the back of the Bible, looked up marriage, and the first thing I came across read, "Wives, submit to your husbands as to the Lord. For the husband is the head of the wife as Christ is the head of the church, his body, of which he is the Savior. Now as the church submits to Christ, so also wives should submit to their husbands in everything."

"I felt as if I'd walked out into the middle of a frozen lake and heard a giant, heart-stopping craaaak *underneath my feet. I didn't want to take a single step until I knew my compass was pointing north."*

You've got to be kidding me, God.

I am a planner who perfectly fits the type A, "born-leader" stereotype. Martin, on the other hand, is a doer. He'd be the first person to tell you that he prefers to operate with rules and direction. Between the two of us, we had divvied up our responsibilities, and we were happy with them. After seven years of marriage we were still best friends. We got along splendidly. Why would we want to upset the applecart?

The question passed out of my mind as quickly as it came in. If I believed that this conversion of faith was real and that the Bible was going to help me to know what to do next, it would stand to reason (or lack of reason) that it was God who was upsetting the applecart. As crazy as it sounded, I was willing to believe that starting on this particular scripture was not a coincidence. I decided to assume that God had led me there and, like it or not, I was to follow.

I've been asked many times since then, "How could you possibly know it was God?" My answer comes in two parts. Part one: I didn't know it was God. I was flying blind and hoping for the best. And really, the things I was doing— reading the Bible, writing in my journal, reading dozens of books by Christian authors, and logging hours of Christian television and radio—were relatively low-risk activities. What was the worst that could happen if I was wrong?

Part two: It had to be God, and the proof was simple—there was absolutely no way that my rational, control-oriented mind would have considered entertaining this silliness a few weeks earlier. I mean, even if my preconversion self had had the impulse to read the Bible, which was highly unlikely, I would have read that line about wives, laughed heartily, and walked away. If I wasn't willing to wake up twenty minutes early to go to church, was I really going to restructure my marriage around words in a book on a lark?

Martin and I had a great marriage and I loved him very much, but I had gone to great lengths in the years following my first marriage to be an independent woman. What possible benefit could come from stepping into some kind of biblical marriage hierarchy in the twenty-first century for no reason, especially when my husband wasn't asking for it? But my postconversion brain seemed to process all input in the direction of doing what I was told, something that was completely out of character. I confronted Martin when he came home that evening.

"Baby," I said in a somber voice. "We need to talk."

"What is it?" he asked, clearly concerned that something else had happened.

"It had to be God. There was absolutely no way that my rational, control-oriented mind would have considered entertaining this silliness a few weeks earlier."

"No worries, honey. It's just that I read the Bible today, and I think that some things need to change around here."

"Like what?" Martin was generally averse to change, and his voice was tentative.

"Well," I said, "I think I have to submit to you."

His concern gave way to a combination of relief and playful aggravation. "What are you talking about?" I know that he used to read the Bible a lot before we met, but I guess this bit must have gone by him.

"If we are going to live this thing, I think we've got to be in it all the way."

"It says it right here. I have to submit to you, and you have to be the head of the household."

Martin looked at me like I had three heads, trying to decide how to respond to this latest wackiness. "Well," he paused, thinking. "I don't want you to submit to me."

"Me, neither. But it says it right here, and if we are going to live this thing, I think we've got to be in it all the way."

I can see now how random this was. And now that I have learned how differently people approach their understanding of what the Bible says to them, and how they react to it, I find this independent choice to respond to this scripture literally is even more fascinating. But this was not some fallible human telling me what I was supposed to do, or a rule some church was throwing down at me. Best I could tell, these instructions were coming from the Big Guy himself, and I was ready to say yes to whatever he put in front of me.

"Okay," Martin said. "Here is my first command."

He certainly shifted quickly from no to yes on this one, I thought, bracing myself for what would come next.

"My first command is . . . that we do everything exactly how we've always done it."

We looked at each other for a moment before we doubled over laughing. And I thought: *God's got his work cut out for him with the two of us.*

I was yet to fully comprehend that this work had begun many years earlier.

CHAPTER SEVEN

Saint Anthony and the Key

F̲ound it!" My friend's voice from the living room left me frozen in place. An unsettling combination of fear and surprise dampened what should have been enthusiasm for the good news.

What the $#@& just happened?

It was 1995, eight years before the day in the church and six months before I attended my first recovery meeting. A half-dozen half-drunk twenty-somethings let up a feeble whoop of relief and headed for the living room, grateful that they could finally stop looking for the ignition key to my car and get back to drinking. I remained in place, confused but certain that something beyond my comprehension had just occurred.

There is no such thing as God . . .

I fought to gain my composure and ground myself in what I knew to be the truth.

There is no such thing as God. And even if there were, God would not reach down from heaven or wherever and find my freaking key . . .

The key in question belonged to a circa 1970 powder-blue Chevrolet sedan that I had been forced to borrow from my uncle a month or two earlier. I should have been more grateful for the loaner, but the pathetic state of my life that necessitated the favor made the whole thing unbearable. If you'd asked me then, I would have sworn that I was far too intelligent and had way too much potential to be living as I was.

On the face of it, the key should have been the least of my worries. With bills to pay and two kids to feed, finding the lost key would normally be little more than a distraction. But I was due to return the car the next morning, and given its age and condition, losing the ignition key was the equivalent of totaling the car.

Incapacitating my uncle's car and the inconvenience it might have caused him were not my primary concerns. No, this was all about me. I couldn't bear to make one more call to my parents to admit yet another irreparable act of irresponsibility. I could already hear the frustrated silence—whispers of their internal dialogue, thinly veiled behind now familiar looks of disappointment, which I interpreted as: *We had such high hopes for you. You started out so well. You had so much potential. Why can't you get your act together?*

I was asking myself the same questions. *Wasn't I supposed to leave high school and become a grand success? Hadn't my early accomplishments been my ticket to a productive and exciting life? Wasn't I destined to make it big?*

I had yet to read the clear indications that I was at the root of my own misery. Casting myself as a victim of bad relationships, bad bosses, bad circumstances, and bad luck was far preferable to admitting defeat, taking a hard look at myself, and seeking help.

> *"I had yet to read the clear indications that I was at the root of my own misery."*

This key had come to mean more to me than whether or not I would be able to return my uncle's car. This small bit of tin, or aluminum, or whatever it is that keys are made of, had become a metaphor for my descent into failure. The final link in a chain of events that shed a blinding light on the expanse between my perceived potential and the place where my actions, attitudes, and choices had taken me.

I had to find this key.

Wasn't there some saint that my grandmother used to pray to, or for, or through when things were lost?

I had no idea where that thought came from. What followed was even more surprising: *Maybe I should pray.*

They were pretty random thoughts, really. I'd never considered prayer to be a sensible response to life's challenges. Truth be told, I had never considered prayer at all. Even when I thought I wanted to be Catholic as a kid, or pursued faith in New Age and Eastern religions in college, I had never thought that faith could involve actually asking God to help me. Looking back, I can see now that I had never really looked for God. I just wanted to be part of something, which made prayer either a waste of time or a quaint but ineffective pastime for gentle women like my grandmother. But we'd been looking for this stupid key for more than an hour, and I was becoming increasingly convinced that we would never find it. So, at age twenty-seven, buzzing nicely on pot and wine, I prayed what was arguably the most pathetic first prayer that has ever been prayed. It went something like this . . .

Okay, I know that there is some saint that my grandmother used to pray to when something was lost. I don't know your name. I don't know what you do, but if you or anyone or anything is out there that can help me, please just find this key . . .

That's when I heard my friend yell, "Found it!" from the other side of the house.

The next few moments play in my head like a bad movie, all chills up the spine and disorientation. I can't say that I immediately believed in God, per se. But I did believe that I had communicated with something and it had responded. Apparently the Queen of the Universe was not alone.

The tiny seed of belief in something beyond myself that was planted that night may have actually been the first step in this fascinating spiritual journey, which eventually led me out of chaos into control, and then to the unpredictable faith that has turned my world upside down years later. Then again, who knows? Maybe it was my parents' simple decision to baptize an unaware six-week-old baby that set my course in motion. Whatever it was, through these two

> *"Buzzing nicely on pot and wine, I prayed what was arguably the most pathetic first prayer that has ever been prayed."*

inexplicable spiritual experiences nearly a decade apart—first the key and then the heart attack that wasn't a heart attack— it had become crystal clear that I was palpably in the radar of a powerful God and that I'd better figure out what that meant.

Wide Awake

I woke with a start—jarred abruptly from a sound sleep—my eyes staring into the pitch-black void of a dark room. It took a moment before I began to focus on Martin's light snoring, a sound that usually bothered me, but that I now found comforting, as it helped to slowly ground me in space.

I am in bed, I told myself. *Martin is here. I am awake.*

Still lying in my bed, I racked my brain to determine what it was that had jolted me from a dead sleep and left me so agitated.

As my eyes adjusted, I could make out the vertical posts of our canopy bed, then the low table on the floor to my left, and the hollowed black gape of the entrance to our master bath on the other side of the room. I would have liked to go right back to sleep. I had work in the morning and had only just gone to bed. But, unfortunately, that was not in the cards. I was awake. Not only that, I was midmorning, two-cups-of-coffee, get-up-and-go awake.

For light sleepers and the bladder challenged, waking up in the middle of the night might be the norm. But Martin and I were incurable night owls, so when I went to sleep, usually after 1:00 A.M., I went to *sleep*. There was no waking me. Disoriented, I turned instinctively toward the dim red glow of the alarm clock that read 3:12 A.M.

Staring at the ceiling, my body motionless and heavy, I began to feel mildly uncomfortable. Like when you leave for vacation and are jarred with the thought that you forgot to lock the front door. I began to wonder, *Did I forget something? Had I been dreaming? Did I leave the stove on?*

I couldn't recall having a dream or nightmare. And since we ordered out for dinner almost every night in those days, the law of averages was on my side regarding the stove. I tried to go back to sleep, but I just couldn't shake this eagerness.

I am supposed to get up. The thought plopped into my head like a stone.

It was early fall, just a few months after that June morning in church, and the room was chilly. I'm one of those people who's always cold, so the idea of following a rogue thought that involved crawling out of a warm bed was out of the question. I pulled the covers up to my chin and ignored the initial impulse. Then I started to argue with myself.

You know you are supposed to get up. I sensed a nudge from God and did my best to ignore it.

I just don't feel like it.

Get up!

Lying there rolled up in Martin and a mass of blankets, I put my foot down to myself. *I will not get up in the middle of the night for no reason.*

Unfortunately, like with the traveler who finally admits that he or she has to go back and check to be sure the front door is locked, the sense that I should get up went from a desire to a need to an unmistakable compulsion.

Oh well, I thought. *I guess I'm getting up.*

Before I knew it, I was squinting against the combined light of the cable box and the alarm clock to find something to put on.

"What are you doing, Joan?" I asked out loud, as I pulled on my robe and tried to get my bearings.

"I put my foot down to myself. I will not get up in the middle of the night for no reason."

I had no answer. Looking back, I probably should have been more concerned about talking to myself, but it seemed normal at the time—that is, if standing in a dark room in the middle of the night waiting for instructions from God can be described as normal. But I quickly became irrationally confident that God was dangling a carrot in front of the nose of this donkey, and I was hungry enough to chase it.

Standing barefoot next to my bed, I pulled the robe a little tighter around my waist and waited. It seemed like there was something I was supposed to do, but I had absolutely no idea what it was. *Okay, God. Here I am. What now?*

Without thinking, I picked up a towel from a short end table that sat next to our bed and folded it—first in half, then in half again. I turned in the darkness and walked slowly, touching down with my toes first to make sure not to trip over the random clothes and shoes that were strewn on the floor of the main area of our eight-hundred-square-foot bedroom, as I made my way toward the hallway, which was flanked by his-and-hers walk-in closets. My hands extended out in front of me to prevent walking into a wall. I felt for the opening that would lead me through the closets into the spare room that we planned to use as a second office when we made the time to furnish it. Apparently that was where I was headed.

When I finally reached the spare room, I placed the towel on the floor mindlessly and descended to my knees. The wood floor was cold and hard, and I toyed with the idea of going back inside to get a blanket. The thought passed quickly, though, as I went from my knees to my stomach in a flash, lying facedown and using the towel as a makeshift pillow. I'd like to say that I was skeptical of this behavior, but even as I hit the floor I continued to be oddly confident that I was on the right track. *Just go with your gut*, I told myself. *Keep doing whatever comes next.* Spreading my arms out on either side of my body like a skydiver, I lay there waiting for something to happen.

Then . . . nothing.

As my ears became acclimated to the silence (Martin and his snoring were thirty-five feet and two closets away), I became aware of other sounds—the wind rustling through the trees outside, a dog barking in the distance. None of it could override the screaming of my internal dialogue.

Okay, God. I'm here and I'm freezing. Now what? I'm not sure if this conversational sense of familiarity was a reflection of my comfort with God or if it betrayed my naiveté about how I should have been addressing the Creator of the Universe. But it was cold, and I was starting to get frustrated. This seemed like a big waste of my time, and I had to figure that if it was a waste of my time, it was probably a waste of God's time as well. Surely God had to have more important things to worry about than me, my towel, and the empty room over my garage.

The committee in my head began to weigh in on what exactly was happening here.

"Maybe you are going nuts," said the curt, cut-to-the-chase part of me.

"Or you need a vacation," said my caretaking, compassionate side.

"I'd been at this God thing for three months. But this was some serious sandwich-board-on-the-corner-wearing, Christian zealot stuff."

"This is ridiculous, you have work in the morning. Go to bed," chimed my voice of reason.

Admittedly, this was a new brand of spiritual wackiness. I'd been at this God thing for three months and was doing my best to follow, listen, and learn. But this was some serious sandwich-board-on-the-corner-wearing, megaphone-holding, the-end-is-near-chanting Christian zealot stuff. This was not the kind of behavior a control freak like me was accustomed to.

But as it became increasingly obvious to me that I was not going to get back into bed until I had some sense of what I was doing there, I was finally able to quiet my objections, and in the silence, I found myself praying: "Dear God, thank you for all that you have given me. For my family, for my job. For our beautiful home. For the grace of knowing you. Please guide my steps, now and always. Increase my faith. Change me. Transform me. Make me something new. Give me wisdom and understanding that I might do whatever it is you have for me to do."

As these gentle, somewhat meditative prayers infused my mind like a pleasant scent, I was enveloped in a penetrating sense of calm. The quiet became just that—quiet.

No dogs barking in the distance. No rustling of trees. No agitation. Even the prayers subsided, leaving me with nothing but an overwhelming sense that everything was going to be okay.

About half an hour, maybe an hour later, I picked up my towel, felt my way along the walls back into the main bedroom, and dove back into bed. There was no big epiphany. No grand enlightenment. No godly to-do list. Just the gift of a quiet moment at the beckoning of the Holy Spirit. Three months earlier I had never contemplated such a thing nor would I have ever thought to ask for it.

The next time this happened was a few weeks later, again at just about 3:00 A.M. and again without warning. This time I knew immediately what it was, so I didn't fight it. I started to get up, but quickly got the impression that I did not have to. Apparently, following set patterns was not part of this Holy Spirit deal. So, instead of lying on the cold, hard floor, I gratefully stayed under the warm covers and prayed until I fell asleep.

———————

They say that it takes about four weeks to make a new behavior a habit, but since that day in June, I had unrelentingly pursued this new faith and showed no sign of returning to my old way of thinking. It was effortless, really. Hours of studying and reading never felt like a chore. Quite the contrary, it was *not* studying or writing or reading that felt unnatural. If I missed a day, I'd actually be disappointed.

It appeared that my initial collision with the Divine had not been a one-time event. My genuine and sustained connection to something beyond myself and the subsequent quest for context for this new relationship had become a constant and consistent part of everything I did. My daytime schedule, which had been weighted heavily in favor of work, house, and family, shifted almost immediately to make room for hours of reading and studying.

> *"It appeared that my initial collision with the Divine had not been a one-time event."*

Instead of hitting the gym before work, I'd set the clock for 6:00 A.M. and park myself at a local café, where I'd sit for an hour or two drinking way too much cappuccino and studying up on this new faith until it was time to head back home to begin my workday. I carried an oversized (and incredibly heavy) bag of journals, books, and Bibles, including a big, thick study Bible with lots of commentary on each page.

I read multiple Bible translations side by side and got my hands on a huge translation dictionary that allowed me to look up words in their original Greek and Aramaic so I could better understand scripture. In addition to my journals, I kept a separate yellow spiral notebook in which I'd track specific questions, insights, and musings.

Working from my home office made it easy to shift my schedule, since I did not have to commute or dress for work unless I was meeting with clients in New York, which was rarely more than once a week. I could wash my face, whip my hair up into a ponytail, throw on a pair of jeans and a T-shirt, and be out of the house and "doing my reading"—as Martin and the kids learned to call it—in less than fifteen minutes.

I was insatiable. In addition to the Bible, there were not enough books or television and radio programs to feed my hunger for knowledge of God, Jesus, and the Holy Spirit. Like a castaway who'd been lost at sea bellying up to the buffet on a cruise ship, I would devour anything and everything I could get my hands on that had to do with Christianity.

Unaware that there were different theological schools of thought, and some pretty radical belief differences among denominations and traditions in the church, I drew from everywhere. I watched television preachers like Joyce Meyer, Joel Osteen, and Creflo Dollar, who talked about God's promises of an abundant life in Jesus Christ. Then I read books by Chuck Swindoll, Beth Moore, and Charles Stanley, who wrote about grace, spiritual disciplines like prayer, and the sacrifices and changes that Christians should pursue if they want to please God and be in right relationship with him.

Later I read people like Rob Bell, Brian McLaren, and Brennan Manning, who talked about a "new kind" of Christianity that focused less on personal changes and more on social justice and embracing broken people and "outsiders." These authors led me to believe that the "old kind" of Christianity must not have done those things very well.

I listened to a Brit on the radio named Derek Prince for months before I realized that he had passed away and these recordings were made in the 1980s. He talked about the Holy Spirit, gifts of the Spirit, and spiritual warfare between Satan, demons, and Christian believers. I read M. Scott Peck, who called for a psychological study on the question of evil in his book *People of the Lie*.

Rick Warren introduced me to the notion that there was a particular, God-inspired purpose for my life, and Henry Blackaby suggested that the best way for me to find it was to go where God was already at work and join in there. Eventually I encountered the early writings of Catholics like Saint Ignatius, Julian of Norwich, Thomas Merton, and Henry Suso, many of whom had written about deep, tangible experiences of God that resonated with me and helped inform my journey.

All in all, I was a spiritual sponge, taking in anything and everything I could get my hands on and cross-referencing it with what I was reading in the Bible. At times I was devouring six or seven books at a time, toggling back and forth between them in random order as my intuition led. (I would later come to believe my "intuition" was actually the guidance of the Holy Spirit.)

"I was a spiritual sponge, taking in anything and everything I could get my hands on."

This hodgepodge of books and authors crossed my path in a variety of ways—a recommendation here, a random choice at the bookstore there—and I learned quickly not to question whether or not they were the "right" books for me. Call it coincidence, but without fail, I found myself encountering the same themes, and sometimes the same scripture passages, in more than one book in the same morning.

If I read a book about grace by one person, say Chuck Swindoll who is an older, rather traditional pastor, I would open a book by Chinese writer Watchman Nee or a more liberal-minded Brian McLaren and read something on the same topic, often related to the same passage of scripture. Later that same day I would turn on the radio or television, and there was Joyce Meyer or Joel Osteen, both popular authors and televangelists, and they would be talking about the same thing. Finally, I'd open the Bible that evening or the next morning and *voilà*, the same passage.

There I'd be, sitting quietly against the wall of the café, peering out from behind a pile of books, grinning from ear to ear as I wandered through these texts and witnessed connection after connection. It was like I was enrolled in some otherworldly theology course taught by an invisible instructor. It was exhilarating. And, of course, it was ludicrous. Yet, as it happened morning after morning, day in and day out, the logic of believing outweighed the logic of not. Despite my best thinking, I couldn't help but grow in confidence that this was more than just coincidence. Something real was happening, and I was compelled to follow it, just as I'd been that first time when God woke me in the middle of the night.

In retrospect, these spiritual calisthenics proved to be critical as I began to develop my prayer life and learn to trust the Holy Spirit of God as a real-time guide rather than as a distant notion. Of course, ignoring the voice of reason and the rest of the thought committee in favor of the voice of the Spirit was counterintuitive, especially for someone with a track

> *"Despite my best thinking, I couldn't help but grow in confidence that this was more than just coincidence."*

record for being as rational and straightforward as I was. Still, I'd soon discover that this going-without-knowing, find-out-when-you-get-there relationship I was developing with the Spirit would eventually lead me to sacrifice a good deal more than an hour or two of sleep.

One of *Them*

Piecing together my first days postconversion is like trying to remember a vivid dream. I know it was intense, but the exact details require some reconstruction. Fortunately, a series of happy coincidences just weeks before my conversion (I like to think of it as some pregrace grace) led me to return to daily journaling for the first time in nearly fifteen years. That is why I will be forever grateful to a friend who, in response to my lament that I could not find time for creative expression in my life, suggested that I read a book by author Julia Cameron, called *The Artist's Way.*

"It really helped me to break free of the things that hold me back from pursuing my artistic self," she told me.

Nice, I thought. *If I don't have time in my busy schedule to pick up my guitar, then I certainly don't have time to read some find-my-inner-artist self-help dreck.*

We were sitting at a small wooden table with four other people at a local restaurant after a midday recovery meeting. This kind of postmeeting coffee klatch is the norm for many of the people who attend recovery meetings, but I was never a fan of small talk. I preferred to get in, get out, and get back to work. For some reason that day was different. Maybe it was someone's birthday or anniversary, but either way I found myself sitting in the same restaurant where I'd smoked cigarettes and drank coffee with my friends on my way to school when I was a teenager, learning how to find my inner Picasso with a table full of recovering addicts.

"Thanks . . . the book sounds excellent," my inner people-pleaser lied in the spirit of cordiality. "I'll definitely check it out."

I would have forgotten about both the book and the conversation had she not walked up and handed me a copy when I saw her a week later. Grateful for the gesture, but still uninterested in the book, I thanked her and threw it on the backseat of my car, where it stayed for a week or two before Martin brought it in and put it on my desk. About a week later I opened it up and tentatively browsed the first couple of chapters. It was that or start a press release for a client, and I was looking for any excuse for procrastination I could find. I never did finish the book. But, fortunately, I got far enough for a bit of nostalgia for my old writing days in college with Darcy to set in. I went out and bought a blank journal the next day.

As with many of the early steps on this ragtag spiritual journey, this reintroduction to journaling seemed inconsequential at the time. Like a grain of sand or a single drop of water, it carried no particular significance and promised no great impact on my day-to-day life. And yet that first journal and more than forty others that I have written since have helped me recall, in sometimes agonizing detail, the deconstruction and continuing reconstruction of my life around a new set of priorities.

Within weeks of my conversion, my journal was peppered with erratic talk of surrender and repentance and desperate pleas to be changed from the inside out. I was driven by something that transcended my own consciousness to listen, follow, and obey. Now, anyone who knew me would have told you that *listen, follow,* and *obey* were not three words they would have associated with me at this time in my life. I was more of a "talk over you, tell you what to do, and go my own way" kind of girl. Yet, some combination of grace and amazement left me with not only the compulsion to obey but also a desire to do so. I wanted to know what God wanted from me, and I was devoted to delivering it, whatever it was. I had a sense that I needed to change, but I did not know what was supposed to change or how I was supposed to get it done.

As I was always one to focus on appearances, some of my biggest worries were the most shallow—like would I have to change my wardrobe. Did being a Christian mean I'd have to wear Christmas-tree sweaters and ugly white blazers with giant fruit or flowers on them? Was I going to have to start wearing flat shoes and nude stockings with navy blue skirts and cardigans buttoned to the neck? What else?

These questions intermingled with deeper, more relevant considerations that filled pages upon pages of meanderings. Would I need to embrace conservative politics and turn away from my friends who are gay or Buddhists?

> *"Within weeks of my conversion, my journal was peppered with erratic talk of surrender and repentance and desperate pleas to be changed from the inside out."*

> *"Did being a Christian mean I'd have to wear Christmas-tree sweaters and ugly white blazers with giant fruit or flowers on them?"*

I wish I could say that my earliest entries make it easy to recall those early days of faith, but even with the help of the journals, memories of the first few weeks after I was "struck" appear as though I am looking at them from a great distance. As with memories of early childhood, I can retrieve a snapshot here and a short scene there, but the chronology is muddy. Instead, there is an ill-defined swirl of conversations, thoughts, and insights that wind around one another. It's like an unstructured, unchoreographed modern dance of images, all set in a cloud of physical agitation, nausea, and punch-drunk enthusiasm. I first attempted to grasp the event in writing about a week and a half after that dramatic Sunday morning when I wrote:

Suddenly it all made sense to me. As promised, more was revealed, and it was overwhelming. I cried during these days. Sometimes I lost my breath. It was then that I realized I was being reborn. I resisted at first. My practical, skeptical self reacted poorly to the notion of being "born again." Seemed cultish to me, and I was embarrassed. I did not want to let anyone know what was happening to me. But, at the same time, I knew that I needed to share it with those who were close to me and eventually with others. But then came the secular me. I should write music, write books, go on speaking tours. From atheist to evangelist in three easy steps. Instead, it became clear that I was to wait. Patiently wait to be led. God has a plan for me. I have willfully turned my back on God and on his will for me for my entire life. Now that I see him, believe in him, trust that he sent his Son to die for us (still a challenge, but I am willing to believe it), I must follow his guidance and wait. More will be revealed, and I am willing to do what I am called to do. I have a feeling, though, that my pride still needs some softening before I am really ready. Only God knows for sure.

Where the $#@& did that come from?

"More to be revealed as promised"? Promised by whom? "During these days"? I was writing about events that had occurred over the past two weeks like it was ancient history. The whole thing was bizarre. And the *"trust that he sent his Son to die for us (still a challenge, but I am willing to believe it)"* part? How could I be Christian without believing in Christ? And yet, despite my hesitation and embarrassment, I knew that what had happened was real and that I somehow believed things in my heart that my mind had not yet absorbed. This encounter had started something in me and left a new faith in its wake. But faith in what?

This is where my path to orthodoxy gets a little unorthodox, although not by design or desire. In fact, there is a part of me that wishes my experience had been more linear, that I saw the light, fell to my knees, accepted Jesus, and could now answer the list of church membership "I dos" and "I don'ts" in the affirmative. That would be so simple, so concrete.

But that was not my experience.

A television fantasy version might have also been

"I somehow believed things in my heart that my mind had not yet absorbed."

nice. One where the clouds part and God whispers to me with a powerful but loving voice (add harps and choirs of cute little Valentine's Day angels here). Jesus whips me up into his arms and I feel a calm, peaceful assurance that everything will be all right.

That wasn't my experience, either.

Never one to do things the easy way, rather than the perfectly ordered conversion or the joy-to-the-world conversion, I got the heart-attacking, nausea-inducing, quaking-in-my-boots, fear-of-God conversion.

Talking about God and fear in the same sentence, I have come to learn, is out of vogue in today's popular Christian vernacular. It is considered a throwback to the days when threats of hell and the call to "turn or burn" (I love that one) were commonplace. This language—and offshoots like sin and repentance—tends to elicit pretty strong reactions one way or the other. Some people bristle when these concepts are discussed, while others believe the Christian message is diluted without them.

Describing my experience as fear does not mean I'm taking a side in this ongoing debate. In fact, while reverential awe and the fear that came with it were indeed the catalysts for this journey, I can't help bristling when the awe of God is used as a tool for manipulation. The whole "do what I tell you or God will punish you for eternity" line doesn't wash with me. Yet an infusion of reverential awe was the way God decided to get my attention, and I can't rewrite my experience to fit my preferred mental concept of who I would like God to be.

Call me a wimp, but getting a supernatural smack-down without asking, praying, or even consciously needing it was scary. Period. Add to that living in limbo between having faith and not knowing what it was that I had faith *in*, and you can't blame me for quaking in my boots a little bit. And yet, with this fear and awe there was a corresponding and perhaps paradoxical (a word I have come to learn defines this faith) sense that this was somehow going to be a good thing. And by good I mean exhilarating. I was excited. I was thrilled. I felt alive—almost high. This sense of anticipation and awe was more roller-coaster fear than lake-of-fire scary. It was also the first hint that my preconceived notion about faith had some pretty big holes in it.

This did not come as a huge surprise to me. While I'd frequently claimed to have read the Bible when I was an atheist, the truth is that I barely skimmed it, and even that was done with no genuine zeal. Unfortunately for Martin and the other people of faith I'd met over the years, I never let the small matter of lack of knowledge stop me from confidently railing against Christianity. And even with limited data, throwing biblical literalists under a bus in a debate was just not that difficult if I could get them to take the bait.

But when I found myself face-to-face with genuine, raw, grace-inspired faith, I quickly recognized that I knew absolutely nothing about what it means to be a follower of Jesus Christ. No reading or documentary could have prepared me. Remember, I'd logged a fair number of church sermons in the years since Martin and I were married, but somehow the story behind the stories had never really sunk in. I knew nothing of the apostle Paul or his miraculous conversion on the road to Damascus. I had no context for why God sacrificed his Son and what that might mean for me in the twenty-first century.

And yet, peeking out from behind this dearth of knowledge was something else. Apparently, this transaction with the

> *"This transaction with the Divine allowed me to believe without knowing the details."*

Divine allowed me to believe without knowing the details. And yet, there was a corresponding hunger for knowledge and action. I somehow *knew* there were things that I was meant to know that I did not yet know, and things I was meant to do that I was not doing, and ways I was supposed to act that I was not acting. Things were going to change.

Throughout this time, a thought kept rolling over in my head like a mantra: *More will be revealed, more will be revealed.* I had no idea what it meant, but it left me with this partly reassuring, partly terrifying sense that God was really out there and that he, she, or it was actually paying attention to me and that I had to face the cold, hard fact that somewhere along the line I had actually become one of *them.*

Unlikely Disciple

"What does it mean when you wake up in the middle of the night and feel compelled to go in the other room, lie on the floor, and pray facedown for half an hour?" I asked Pastor Thomas as we sat facing each other in his office at the church. The spines of books that filled the floor-to-ceiling shelves on the wall behind my wooden chair provided the only character to the small, square room that was overly full of mismatched office furniture, flip charts, and piles of remnant materials from Bible studies and kids camps. We were sitting in what appeared to be a cement-block extension on the older, magnificent fieldstone structure that housed the main sanctuary where I'd had my conversion experience months earlier. He'd been meeting with me there once a week for the past couple of months, answering my questions and offering suggestions as I tried to make some sense of what had happened to me.

I'd shared the story of my conversion with Pastor Thomas a few weeks after it happened, hoping that he might provide me with some context for this event. His face had betrayed no particular emotion as I reconstructed the experience for him, detail by detail.

Pastor Thomas listened carefully without speaking as I tried to find words to explain the heart attack that wasn't a heart attack and the compulsion to study and learn that had followed it. Halfway through the story he stood up, crossed the room, and, standing slightly behind me to my left, began scanning his bookshelves as I was speaking.

"Would you like me to wait?" I asked, partly to be polite and partly because I was mildly insulted that I did not have his full attention. Though I was on the road to acknowledging that the world did not revolve around me, I certainly hadn't reached my destination.

"No, no," he said in an absentminded tone that bordered on dismissive. "Keep going, I'm listening."

And I did, attempting to reconstruct the blurry first days, describing the frequency of my serendipitous reading experiences and the details of my encounters with people at the café and elsewhere.

"The weird thing about these connections in my reading," I told him, "is that they are also connected to people."

He turned from the books. "What do you mean?"

I told him about the scripture coincidences and how the things I read seemed to come up over and over again from different sources. "Then," I continued, "I run into somebody I know, or sometimes a stranger, who brings up something that relates directly to the same exact topic. I share what I just learned and inevitably they tell me it was 'just what they needed to hear.'"

"Go on," Pastor Thomas encouraged me, turning from the bookshelves and picking up a legal-size yellow notepad where he took some sporadic notes.

"The rest happens differently each time," I told him. "But eventually they wind up either trying to give me credit for the information or asking me where I learned it." I didn't know much at this stage of the game, but I had no intention of taking credit for this newly implanted wisdom. "That's when the spiritual 'six degrees of Kevin Bacon' game starts."

He looked up from the notebook with a blank stare that left me with the impression that he was not familiar with the Kevin Bacon game.

"Well, Kevin Bacon has been in lots of movies with lots of stars." *What's up with me, explaining the Kevin Bacon game to a pastor?* I wondered as I spoke. "So, if you start with any actor, you can trace your way back to Kevin Bacon in six moves or less."

He said he understood my explanation, but the glazed-over look in his eyes contradicted him. "Anyway, my conversion story is like some spiritual version of the six degrees of Kevin Bacon game. No matter what I am talking about, all roads lead back to my encounter with God." By now I was speaking excitedly. "Sometimes this happens in two or three conversations with wildly different people on the same day."

His posture relaxed, "Well, that makes sense." His tone told me that he was expecting a curveball, but that—once he'd gotten past the Kevin Bacon nonsense—I'd pitched him one that he could hit out of the park. "Many people who come to faith have an enthusiasm for sharing it with others; that is a good thing. Nothing to worry about."

"No, you don't understand." I may have sounded frustrated, but not with him. Finding words to capture these experiences was a challenge for me. Still is. It's like trying to describe the sound of wind chimes in the distance on a summer day or the rich tone of a C-sharp chord strummed on a Les Paul guitar.

"*I* don't bring it up to *them; they* bring it up to *me*." My inner fourteen-year-old was jumping up and down screaming, *Why won't you listen to me?* But he was listening—I was just trying to describe the indescribable.

"Let me try to explain what it is that I mean."

I went on to tell him how, within weeks of my conversion, I continually encountered people whose personal experiences and challenges were directly related to some new insight I had recently gleaned from my prayer time and my studies. This wasn't a one-off or occasional thing. It happened almost every day. In some cases, it was a direct connect. I'd be sitting in the café and someone would walk up and ask me what I was reading.

> "*It's like trying to describe the sound of wind chimes in the distance on a summer day or the rich tone of a C-sharp chord strummed on a Les Paul guitar.*"

"Just doing some studying," would be my first response. I hate to admit it, but when I saw someone coming over, I would frequently cover the titles of my books or subtly pile them in such a way that people could not see what I was reading. I still wasn't 100 percent comfortable about this Bible-reading-in-public business, but it was where I believed I was supposed to do it; and like the night in my room, I was getting into the habit of following these Holy Spirit impulses, whether I liked them or not.

"Oh, what are you studying?"

Unintentionally employing my PR skills to answer and, at the same time, avoid the question, I'd reply, "Just some spiritual stuff about . . ." and I would fill in the blank with a topic like worry or marriage or whatever it was that the Spirit was leading me to hone in on that day.

I'd never lead with the Bible or Jesus or anything related to my conversion. And yet, whether I had my books on the table in the café or I was on the telephone with someone on a completely different matter, the person's questions and comments would persist until I faced a choice: either take credit for an insight that they were somehow praising me for or give credit where credit was due.

"Well, I was reading the Bible and . . ." I'd finally admit, like they'd caught me stealing. And that was all it took. It seemed like everyone I met had a story to tell about Christianity. Many had given up on the church or turned to a different religion, or like me, had never embraced religion at all. But, whatever the story, they wanted to talk about it. And I listened, amazed at how similar the stories were and how intensely they wanted to share them. I had little context for their church troubles, but it was clear that many of them had been hurt or disappointed by their experiences with faith. Then, once they had gotten that out, the topic would turn back to me.

"What about you?"

And there I'd be yet again, the reluctant evangelist, looking down, shaking my head, and wondering how it could possibly be happening again: my telling my conversion story to someone I barely knew or, even worse, someone I had known for years. Every time, as the story unfolded, something would change in me. My reluctance would give way to an enthusiasm and brightness that seemed to emanate from a place deep within me and burst forth like an explosion. That same conversion-day pressure would mount behind my sternum, but

"People would show up, one after the other: some Christians, others Buddhists, agnostics, atheists, people in recovery—you name it."

now without the distress. I could feel my eyes brighten and my smile widen as I spoke of it without inhibition, enjoying every minute of it.

There were some days when I would sit at the table in Caffe a la Mode, one of my favorite study spots, feeling like Lucy in the Charlie Brown comics. The spiritual doctor is in! People would show up, one after the other: some Christians, others Buddhists, agnostics, atheists, people in recovery—you name it. Their beliefs didn't seem to matter a bit. Each would have a different story with a different set of circumstances, and yet something from the bit of scripture or a book I'd been reading would resonate with them in a way that felt profound to them and to me.

We'd talk, sometimes for five minutes and other times for five hours. I never knew when we began just how long one of these conversations might last. The people almost always got something out of it, or so they'd say, and they would leave, thanking me profusely for all of my help.

Thanks for my help? I thought. Half the time I was saying things and sharing insights that I hadn't had before. I'd start with a story I'd heard on Christian TV that morning or a parable I'd read in the Bible, and describe its connections to other readings or experiences that would emerge as I spoke. I think that was part of the reason I began to accept that something beyond me was going on. I was amazed that these profound insights— far more profound than I could reach on my own—would spew out of my mouth. None that wouldn't be familiar to students of the great spiritual thinkers, but they were all new to me.

Sure, I was always a high achiever, but I just wasn't that deep a thinker. There were times when I'd actually interrupt myself to grab a napkin or sheet of paper to write down what I'd just said, so I could refer back to it later. I usually ended these conversations feeling invigorated until, like someone who is in shock, I would crash under the weight of a combination of embarrassment and physical and mental exhaustion a few minutes after I finished speaking.

"I am so sorry for being so intense," I would tell them, asking myself why I couldn't just keep my big mouth shut and promising myself that I wouldn't do *that* again. But they didn't seem to mind. Even the ones who had been bashing the church ten minutes earlier would hear me out. "No, don't apologize," they would reassure me. "I remember feeling like that about God," they'd say. Or sometimes it was, "I've never felt that way about God." Or, "That's not the Christianity I learned about in Sunday school." Whatever their responses, I didn't try to change their minds. I just shared my story, admitting that I had no idea what I was doing. I was just going with it.

I found it all very exciting and very strange. I'd come home to Martin, talking a blue streak. "You are not going to believe what happened. I ran into so-and-so today, and she asked me about such and such. Then I told her I'd just read . . ."

I went on and on. I am surprised he didn't shoot me.

Instead, although patience is not Martin's strong suit, he listened and encouraged and questioned my interpretations of these encounters. As a lifelong Christian who had never had this sort of experience of God himself, Martin became a welcome (although sometimes frustratingly practical thinking) sounding board for my less than practical journey. He kept me grounded, and his simple wisdom frequently led me back to the drawing board. That's when I would drag out the Bibles and the translation dictionary, and really try to dig in deep on the topic.

I told Pastor Thomas all of this, hoping he might be able to help me.

At our first meeting, he didn't say much. He just handed me some books he had collected from the shelves as we spoke and suggested that I check them out to see if anything resonated with me. Then, he called out through the open door to the church secretary, who was sitting at her desk in a large foyer. I'll call her Pat.

"Pat," he shouted, still not looking away from the bookshelves as if there was something else there that he was looking for. "Can you please find a time that Joan can come by once a week?"

Thus began the formal part of my Christian education.

I'd spend my week reading, studying, and chronicling my encounters, and would return to Pastor Thomas's office with long lists of questions.

"Well." He listened intently and chose his words carefully when he finally responded. "I'm not too sure what the waking up and being compelled to walk into the other room is all about, but I can tell you that there are several prayer postures described in the Bible." He flipped through his Bible silently, holding up his index finger to shush me as he turned pages looking for scriptures. He'd then pluck out passages that described people standing, sitting, kneeling, and lying in prone positions to pray and worship. As he blurted them out,

I would scribble down the chapter and verse numbers in my spiral notebook so I could dig into them on my own.

"I'd spend my week reading, studying, and chronicling my encounters, and then I would return to Pastor Thomas's office with questions."

Each week my questions would guide the conversation. As we spoke, he'd stand in front of that same bookshelf until he'd zero in on a book or study that he thought might inform the next step of my journey.

"Why don't you take a look at this," he'd say, handing me a book or a binder or a Bible study without turning from the shelves. Inevitably these materials would dovetail with others that I had acquired through different means, further confirming that there was something universal happening here. Pastor Thomas agreed and was enthusiastic in his support of my journey. Pat would laugh as I'd walk out of his office, my bag laden with books and notes and scripture references, which I would devour before our next meeting.

Eventually I shared my story with Pat, a devout woman whose knowledge of the Bible and gentleness were inspiring. She and I sang together in the church band, and eventually participated in group Bible studies together, so my weekly session became double tutelage: meeting informally with Pat outside the office before or after my sessions with Pastor Thomas and then "officially" with him. I went on like this for more than a year.

I'd love to take credit for all of this spiritual zeal, to hold myself up as some wonderful example of what all Christians could or should do if they were just as holy and devout as I was. But that would be both obnoxious and misleading. Left to my

> *"I was compelled to act—was led toward a transformed life, and I could not imagine countermanding it."*

own devices, I would have turned my back on this long, long ago. But the combined effect of this transforming faith—the constant confirming coincidences, and the urging that would well up inside of me like a volcano until I was compelled to act—was leading me toward a transformed life, and I could not imagine countermanding it.

I was committed. Submitted. Desperate to hear more, learn more, and do more. At some level I must have known that I had free will, but I could not imagine saying no. It might sound like a horrible experience to some people, and in the not too distant past I would have been one of them, but I never felt burdened or put-upon. I wanted to follow. Despite a lifetime of striving for independence and autonomy, I readily and happily chose to obey.

Illusion of Control

It was into this somewhat magical spiritual honeymoon that a single, radical thought began to buy up real estate in my mind.

You need to quit your job.

Quit my job? I'd recently been promoted to vice president of a small public-relations firm, and one of the owners and I had discussed the future possibility of a partnership. I was making a very comfortable six-figure salary and the benefits were great. *Why would I want to quit my job?*

For some people, quitting work might seem like a dream come true, but not me. I loved work. I'd held one job or another since I was twelve years old. Ten, if you count babysitting. I had put myself through college, working three jobs to do it, and I'd juggled several others when the kids were little. I fell into the public-relations business in the early 1990s, through an underdog political campaign that had unexpectedly resulted in a win and a job offer: press secretary cum administrative assistant for a county-government official. This, my first consistent, full-time position since my fall from high-achiever grace, was my second chance—the opportunity I needed to get my career back on track and fulfill the potential that had been predicted all those years ago.

I came into that job like a barracuda—which had good and bad outcomes. I was a twenty-seven-year-old know-it-all nightmare who had everything figured out and wasn't worried about stepping on toes to let people know it—including the elected official I worked for. I wince when I think back about myself in those years. I was doing my best to create a façade of professionalism and competence, when in reality I was one step out of the chaos of a failed marriage and away from the days when I hadn't been able to pay my bills.

Despite my aggressive style, I had just enough experience, diligence, and smarts to pull it off. I also had enough to turn the head of a communications director for a Fortune 500 company who did business with the municipality. I'll call him Doug. We'd had occasion to work together on some emergency planning projects, and less than two years after I took the county position, Doug hired me as a communications manager.

Contrary to my impression that Doug's motivation for hiring me had everything to do with my newly acquired communication skills, he admitted years later, when he spoke at the anniversary of my first year in sobriety, that it was something else he saw in me. He was fourteen years sober when I met him in 1994, and without ever seeing me drink, he came to believe that I had a problem with booze and that he was

> *"I was doing my best to create a façade of professionalism and competence, when in reality I was one step out of chaos."*

supposed to point me in the direction of the people who could help me solve it.

Thank God he saw it, because I had no idea.

I knew that I liked to drink, and my college days were not so far behind me that I could not recall the chaos that resulted from it. But I'd simmered down on the hard stuff, and since I'd accepted the government job, I'd even stopped smoking pot (well, kind of—unless I was at a party or on vacation).

I was not one to drink or get high before the kids went to bed. In fact, I was particular about having all of my ducks in a row (or at least stuffing things in the closet and creating the impression of ducks in a row) before I would pour a drink or light up a joint in the evening. And anyway, if I had a problem, so did everyone I knew. Almost everyone I came into contact with partied the way I did—some even worse.

These were the lies about my drinking and drug use that had become my truth as I'd watched my potential separate from my reality like oil from water in my early to mid-twenties. I'd never considered the possibility that I was using alcohol and drugs to mask a host of insecurities and social disconnects, or that, in doing so, I had stunted my emotional and spiritual growth.

Fortunately, unbeknownst to me, God appeared to conspire against my addiction and my misery by bringing people like Doug and Martin into my life at the same time as I found that key and began to recognize that the world might be different from the rigid mold I had cast it to be. In-

> "I'd never considered the possibility that I was using alcohol and drugs to mask a host of insecurities and social disconnects."

terestingly, my moment of truth, my bottom, came on the day in 1995 when Martin, whom I was dating, and Doug, who was helping me to build a career, both threatened to give up on me.

I did not sign up for this," Martin told me as I walked in the door at 10:00 P.M. It was the first he had seen or heard from me since I'd left work five hours earlier. We were not yet married, but taking Martin's generosity for granted, I assumed correctly that he would pick up Andrew and Kelsey from the babysitter and put them to bed.

"I know, I know," I said, head in my hands and wondering how this could be happening: Martin calling me on my irresponsibility at the same time as Doug was suggesting that I would need to make some changes if I wanted my circumstances to change.

Earlier that evening I had met with my ex-husband, who then lived overseas, a couple of blocks from my office to finalize some paperwork. We had been legally separated for nearly two years and the divorce was just about final. I was upset after the meeting, as I always was when I met with my ex-husband. So, resorting to what I did not yet realize was my go-to coping mechanism, I drank five rye Presbyterians, my not-so-ironic drink of choice (rye whiskey, ginger ale, and soda), in the twenty minutes between finishing with the ex and getting in the car with Doug, who had agreed to give me a ride home.

Doug had shared with me months before that he was a sober alcoholic who used to drink whiskey. He was livid.

"How dare you get into my car drunk and reeking of whiskey!" he screamed. He went on to paint a vivid picture of how selfish and self-centered and arrogant I was and that, while he had hoped to help me, I was beyond help, and he was not going to let me drag him down with me.

I was livid, too.

"Who do I think *I* am? Whoduyah think *you* are?" I said, slurring my speech slightly. My head was spinning, not from the drinks but from the situation. *What is happening here? What is he talking about?* I had not known until that car ride that Doug, without ever having seen me drink, thought I had a problem with alcohol, and that his decision to offer rides home and support with work were part of his recovery program. Looking back on it, I can't believe I didn't see that something was up. He bent over backward for me and never asked a thing from me in return. But I had never once considered that I had anything to recover from, and I had no familiarity with his or any other 12-step program.

He drove me to the train station near my house, where I had parked my car that morning. We spent almost four hours sitting in his car, talking about recovery and addiction. Despite throwing back five drinks in twenty minutes because I'd had a bad day (and it would have been more if time had allowed), I still was not convinced that I had a problem. But I listened to what Doug had to say and admittedly recognized some of myself in the stories he shared with me.

One after the other, he told me about intelligent, high-achieving people whose lives had crumbled under the weight of their unrelentingly self-sabotaging behavior. The rise and fall of the lives of the addicts he described looked nothing like my sleeping-in-a-box-on-the-street mental image of addicts. In fact, they sounded a lot like me. Could it be that all of these years of fighting against myself was related in some way to my use of drugs and alcohol? I wasn't ready to admit the possibility, but a seed had been planted. Finally, I went home where Martin, who lived across town from me, was waiting for me with my kids.

I am sure he knew that I had been drinking, although I had sobered up hours earlier.

"Where were you?" he asked, half-worried that something had happened to me and half-angry that I was just fine.

I didn't know what to say. I didn't want to admit that I'd been talking about sobriety; I knew that, while my conversation with Doug was on the up-and-up, it certainly didn't sound good to tell my boyfriend that I had spent the last four hours in the car with my male boss. Doug was at least twenty years older than me and happily married with kids, but still. Rather than stick with the truth, I chose to make up an elaborate story, and it was a whopper.

"Well," I said apologetically, knowing that he was beyond angry now that he knew I was not hurt or worse. "I was so upset after the meeting that I decided to go to Washington Square Park to buy some pot. Then I sat on a bench and got high and sat there for a few hours by myself just thinking."

Martin looked at me silently for at least a minute. I am not sure what he did or did not believe, since, unfortunately, sitting alone in the park getting high is something that I might have actually done on another day. But, true or false, he had been waiting in my house for hours, taking care of my children while I was out doing something without the courtesy of a telephone call. It didn't matter what I was doing. This was unacceptable, and Martin had had enough. That's what he meant when he said, "I didn't sign up for this."

As with many addicts, my bottom was not the worst night of my life. I'd faced far worse situations than this and made my way out the other end. But on this night, facing down the disgust and anger of these two men, a glimmer of reality snuck in behind my armor. Like a distant whisper, the question rose from the depths of my soul.

"I was so used to assigning blame to circumstances and bad luck that I had never considered that there might be something broken in me."

Could I be the problem here?

I was so used to assigning blame to circumstances and bad luck that I had never considered that there might be something broken in me that needed fixing. And it took years more for me to comprehend the deception of mind and abject self-reliance that made me believe smoking a joint in the park was a better story than admitting I might actually need help.

I attended my first recovery meeting at 8:00 A.M. the following Saturday. I went to Doug's home group, which met two hours from my house in Connecticut. And while it took me several weeks of attending meetings as a skeptic, I eventually came to accept that I wanted what these folks had. With the help of the people I met in recovery and the guidance of an ill-defined higher power, I began to change.

By hearing the hard stories of other self-destructive people who had found a way to get beyond their worst enemy—themselves—I learned about the importance of humility and the power of prayer. I began to learn about letting go and allowing something bigger than myself to do for me what I had been unable to do for myself. Eventually I shared my story and allowed the God of the car keys to come alive in my life and transform me into a more responsible person. As I began to practice the recovery principles in my day-to-day life, I began to change.

Martin supported me fully, and we were married a year later. With the help of recovery and the strength of a new marriage, my career took off. I spent several more years working for Doug and then I jumped into the dot-com business before landing at the PR agency where I was working when I had my conversion experience.

———————

My career, which recovered as I recovered, had been hard won. How could it be that now, after coming to a faith in God, after finally pulling together the life I had always wanted—the life I *deserved*—God was telling me to quit my job? This had to be wrong.

The first time leaving my job came to mind was in the midst of a stream-of-consciousness rant in my journal, which was typical for my morning writing sessions. I filled these journals with everything from conversations to prayers, observations, questions, song lyrics, poetry—whatever came to mind as I turned my attention to God. That morning, as I wrote about my purpose and committed myself for the hundredth time to "do whatever you want me to do, Lord," I wrote the words, "You need to quit your job."

I stopped and stared at my own writing as if someone else had snuck into my journal and left a bit of graffiti there.

You need to quit your job?

This was too much. It was all fun and games to follow God into the spare room at 3:00 A.M. and to meet with Pastor Thomas at the church, and even to speak with these people in the café who seem to need some help—but quit my job? No wonder I felt the need to let this thought, which never left me, percolate for a couple of weeks before I told Martin what was on my mind.

"What makes you think you are supposed to quit?"

It was a reasonable question.

"It is hard to describe," I told him. "I can't put my finger on it, but I really think I am supposed to do it. I'm just not sure when or how."

Think *Alice in Wonderland*: When the note said "Drink Me," Alice drank. When it said "Eat Me," she ate. She didn't know if she'd shrink or grow or get swept up in a salty river of her own tears. But somehow it didn't matter. The possibilities of what lay on the other side of the task were so compelling that it was worth the risk.

But thinking that I was *supposed* to do it didn't exactly translate to *wanting* to do it. I mean, leaving my career was taking this obedience thing to another level.

While I may have read it, I hadn't connected yet with the part in the Bible where Jesus asks a couple of his soon-to-be apostles to come on the road with him. These guys were midway through their workday, and this guy just rolls into town and asks them to follow. And they do. No questions asked. They just drop their nets and follow him. While I might have been comforted by that story if I'd known about it, I still couldn't help but wonder what God had to gain by poking around in my career. In some ways, the reason did not matter. All I

> *"The possibilities of what lay on the other side of the task were so compelling that it was worth the risk."*

knew was, as with that first night when I sensed that I was supposed to get out of bed and pray, the thought that I had to quit my job, which had begun as a whisper, was now a roar.

Apparently this change of faith was going to be accompanied by a corresponding change in lifestyle.

So a month or more after I first wrote the words in my journal, Martin and I sat down at the kitchen table and seriously discussed it.

"What would you do?" Martin asked. I had worked since he'd known me.

"I don't know. Study. Write. Whatever comes up."

Martin, who owned his own business, was thinking practically. "What about health insurance?" This was an important question with three children.

"I don't know; maybe we can create an employee policy through your business."

Martin's business was strong enough to cover the household expenses, and we had a very comfortable buffer of savings and investments. We were used to having lots and lots of money floating around, but half of lots and lots would still keep us comfortable. We'd have to lighten up our discretionary spending, but we agreed that was likely a good thing.

All in all, if we tightened our belts a little (which was relative, since we would still be bringing in more than $100,000 a year with Martin's business), it was financially feasible for us to follow God. I am sure God was just thrilled to learn that our numbers worked in his favor.

Despite coming to the conclusion that we *could* do it, I didn't quit right away. There were two things holding me back. First, while I was confident that I was being prompted to leave my job, I was not clear about timing. When I'd woken up in the middle of the night to pray or had those conversations in the café, I knew I was supposed to do it *now*. In this case, however, I felt more like a girl standing on the edge of a jump rope. I knew I was going in, but I watched it turn over and over again, waiting for the perfect time to take that step. I'd like to say that my hesitation was all wrapped up in a desire to please God—waiting for his timing so I would pull the trigger on cue. But there was another, more selfish reason I had not pulled the trigger. I didn't *want* to quit my job.

Walking away from my job meant more than walking away from my salary and benefits; I was walking away from my identity. I liked my work. I liked making my own money. And I liked the prestige associated with being a VP at a PR agency. I liked sitting across the table from a client whose CEO was demanding results on a media campaign and coming up with the tactic or strategy that made it work. My work was not just a vocation, it was who I was. If I quit work, I'd face a double whammy: being dependent on Martin for money and losing my identity.

Depending on Martin was not so much of a problem. While I had vowed to never put myself in the position of relying on any man ever again after my failed first marriage, the unlikely outcome of that little "I'm supposed to submit to you" Bible marriage experiment allowed me to dismiss that concern surprisingly easily. By embracing, rather than

> *"Having long defined myself by what was on the business card, walking away from my job meant more than walking away from my salary and benefits."*

ignoring, it I'd already figured out that "submitting" to Martin didn't mean he says *jump* and I say *how high?* It meant learning to trust him, and I was getting much better at that.

Which left the prestige problem. Who would I be without my title and my salary? I knew it wasn't true, but a part of me felt that without my career to define me I might just disappear. I never realized how much my sense of self was tied to my job until I faced losing it. And this wasn't just *losing* it; I was *giving it away*. I faced a choice: follow an uncertain path in pursuit of a life with this God or pursue a lucrative career. I don't believe for a moment that following Jesus necessitates this kind of a radical abandonment of career for everyone, but for some reason, God was asking me to take this counterintuitive step.

I wrote endlessly on the subject in my journals. Putting my thoughts down on paper allowed me to examine them more clearly. I was split. My gut and my brain were at odds with each other. It was as if everything I had ever thought or learned needed to be pulled out and examined through the lens of this new faith, and I was frequently drawn to the least logical place. Bantering back and forth with myself on the lined sheets in front of me one morning, I found a question staring back at me.

What if you are wrong?

What if I was starting to give too much credence to these "leadings" and I was starting to lead myself? How could I know for sure that it was God's voice that I was hearing? I wanted some kind of a sign that

> "What if I was starting to give too much credence to these 'leadings' and I was starting to lead myself?"

never came. So, in lieu of a lightning bolt from heaven, Martin and I made a random call. We decided that I would leave work the following summer. That would give us six months to save some money and prepare for the change. It seemed like a reasonable approach, and we put the job thing on the shelf. Unfortunately, circumstances began to indicate that our "guestimate" on the timetable was a little off.

Saying Yes

Standing in the kitchen on a Monday in October, four months into my conversion experience and about a month after I'd begun to think that I was being prompted by God to leave work, I heard a boom and then a blunt *thud* coming from one of the kids' rooms on the second floor, and I took off running.

In moments like these I can observe the animal instinct part of motherhood—that part of me that would put myself in front of a bullet for one of my kids. Unfortunately, it sometimes took a metaphorical bullet for that part of me to come to the surface. With or without a crisis, I always loved my children. It's just that expressing or accepting love was never my strong suit.

You could count on me to be loyal. You could count on me to work hard and to provide for you. But emotionally, I could be pretty unavailable. There are a million reasons that this might be the case, and I am sure there are some armchair psychologists out there who would love to take a stab at it. Whatever the reasons, I can look back at my earliest memories and see that I always felt separate and distinct in my interactions with people.

———————

I wish I could get back into my four-year-old head, to know what I was thinking when I decided to run away from home. We were still in Brooklyn at the time, in a house on Colman Street about ten blocks from my grandmother's house, where my mother grew up. None of us seems to remember what it was that set me off, but my decision was made. I was moving out. I don't remember packing the little suitcase, although I have a snapshot recollection of carrying it up the stairs from my basement bedroom, through the dining room and living room to the front door. The suitcase was round and hard-sided, like a hatbox, with a clasp to keep it closed and a loop handle. In my memory it was huge, but it was probably made to carry doll clothes, not my wardrobe for starting a new life.

It must have been spring or summer, since I cannot remember putting on a coat. My parents let me go, finding the whole thing cute and wondering how far I would take it before I'd turn around and come back. I am sure they thought I wouldn't make it farther than the front stoop, or maybe the corner, but they sent my older brothers, who were eight and nine at the time, to follow me.

I should add that it was the early 1970s (I was born 6/6/66, a hoot for Bible numerology buffs and fans of the movie *The Omen*). In those days, kids went out to play by themselves for hours on end, until they heard a whistle or whatever call was agreed upon to mean *get home now*. Our parents always knew *approximately* where we were, but rarely *exactly* where we were. Even so, we were rarely on our own. These were the days when every adult you encountered was your parent. If you were acting up or being disrespectful, any adult would call you on it without fear of reprisal. They might even grab you by the shirt collar and walk you home to tell your parents what it was that you did or did not do.

In this environment, sending an eight- and nine-year-old to follow a four-year-old runaway didn't seem as strange as it might today. Of course, I had no idea that my brothers were hiding behind a parked car and watching me when I approached the corner. I may have turned to see if my parents were watching—but maybe not. What I do know is that this tiny, freckle-faced girl with two blond pigtails and a suitcase looked both ways, as she had been taught, and crossed that street. Then I crossed the next one. And the next one, all the way to my grandmother's house. Brave. Independent. Risk taker. These characteristics were there from the beginning and they punctuated my interactions with people. I didn't need my parents. I didn't need my brothers. I didn't need anyone.

And yet, there was a paradox.

As the years passed and I continued to portray myself as a loner, the people around me responded in kind. Why dote on the person who has it all covered? I began to see that I did desire closeness with people. I wanted to be a part of things— but only on my own terms. I was a double-sided emotional magnet, both attracting and repelling people as I flipped from side to side. I had a desire to be part of a social community, but I never wanted those relationships to go deep or become intimate. In my perfect world, I would receive and give love when I felt inspired to do so, always maintaining the option

> *"I did desire closeness with people. I wanted to be a part of things— but only on my own terms."*

of retreating, at my convenience, without consequence. Naturally, I did not recognize this tendency in myself.

Caught up in the "doing" side of life, whether that meant doing things right or doing them wrong, I had rarely, if ever, thought about the "being" side of life.

The same went for my family. My husband and kids could count on me to work hard for them, but when it came to that one-on-one talking about the school day or commiserating on a hard day at work, I had little patience for "being" there for them. I tried. But, even when I was sitting there looking them straight in the eye, I often found myself lost in thought—less looking *at* them than staring *through* them.

———————

Crises engaged the "doing" part of me, so when I heard that *thump* through the ceiling, I hit the stairs two at a time, calling for Andrew, who was the only one home at the time.

"What was that?" I shouted down the hall, unsure what I would encounter as I turned the corner into his room. He was flat on his back, eyes open but looking dazed.

"Andrew, what happened? Talk to me. What happened?" I was trying to rouse him. I'd never used smelling salts, but it seemed as if they were made for a moment like this. All I had was my hands and my voice.

"Andrew," I said sternly as I lightly slapped his cheek. "Wake up."

"Fell," he said, his voice giddy but his face concerned like a dental patient on laughing gas whose teeth hurt.

In the weeks prior, Andrew had been complaining on and off about having "head rushes" when he got up from the couch. He'd described these episodes as the lightheaded feeling you get when you stand up or bend down too quickly. Admittedly, I didn't take it very seriously at first. He was fourteen years old and growing like a weed. I just told him to drink more water, take vitamins, and stand up slowly. But now, bent over him and looking at the glassy, distant look in his eyes, I knew that this was something more than growing pains.

I helped him to the bed and kept watching his eyes. I had heard horror stories about seemingly minor head injuries that wound up fatal, and a five-foot-eight-inch, 165-pound teenager has a long way to fall when he is toppling over like a tree. I didn't want to take any chances. For another kid, drugs might have been a possible explanation but it didn't even cross my mind with Andrew. It wasn't that he was beyond wrongdoing, but in those days partying wasn't his style. Dozens of toxicology reports over the coming months confirmed my initial impression: neither drugs nor alcohol had been a factor.

I called my sister, an emergency-room nurse, who told us to keep a close eye on him for the next twenty-four hours, and bring him straight to the hospital if anything seemed strange. She also suggested a specialist, whom I called the next morning to make an appointment.

"I knew that this was something more than growing pains."

Thankfully, Andrew's head was fine, but the "head rushes" were getting worse. By the time we got him to the right doctor a week or two later, he couldn't stand up without blacking out. We called the school, collected his work, and kept him home for the days and weeks it took us to find some answers.

Being able to work and care for Andrew, Kelsey, or Ian when they were home sick from school was one of the biggest perks of my PR job. I had created a home office that rivaled those I'd been assigned when I'd done corporate work. There were two large mahogany desks on opposite walls, one for Martin and one for me. Mine faced two large windows and was flanked by a state-of-the-art computer printer, file cabinets, and a wall of wooden bookshelves that were filled with reference texts, office supplies, and anything else I needed to make working from home convenient and professional.

Since my firm was completely virtual, we had no central office. Each employee operated from a home office and we coordinated our work by telephone, e-mail, and in coffee shops and restaurants on either side of client meetings, which were scheduled once or twice a month. Once a quarter, the entire staff of the company would come together at rented space in New York or Connecticut, to discuss broad strategic issues and put names to faces. This virtual-office setup is common practice for many companies today, but in 2000 it was downright avant-garde. In fact, we were asked to maintain a don't-ask, don't-tell policy with our clients about the fact that we did not, technically, "report to work."

This business model was made-to-order for a woman like me. I didn't mind working with people; it was a means to an end. I just didn't want to hang out with them. I found office parties and small talk over coffee annoying and time wasting. As far as I was concerned, work was about working, not socializing. With this setup, coworkers weren't tempted to pop their heads in my office and ask a stupid question or sit down and share their life story. We did conference calls once a week, communicated by e-mail during the day, and members of my account teams could always call me if they needed anything. Otherwise, everyone was on his or her own.

I'd never had a job before or since in which I got so much work done. Except for client calls, I was able to focus for hours at a time, without distraction.

This schedule didn't change much when one of the kids was home sick. I'd set them up in the family room with a blanket, some juice, the remote, and a phone, so they could call me if they needed something. This allowed me to be in two places at once. It was ideal.

But something changed in me as Andrew's condition became chronic.

We thought he had it licked when the passing out was explained by a condition called POTS (postural orthostatic tachycardia syndrome), which resulted in blood pooling in his abdomen when he stood up. Fortunately, it was easily remedied with a blood-pressure medication that had few reported side effects. He was able to return to school after a few days on the medicine, and things got back to normal. But not for long.

Less than two weeks later, new symptoms started to pop up. The "head rushes" were merely the first in a slew of troubling physical symptoms that a spectrum of doctors were having a hard time diagnosing. As a result, Andrew lost almost half a year of school and was in and out of the hospital more than a half dozen times over an eighteen-month period.

Martin and I did our best to use sick days and creative scheduling to fill the gaps between what Andrew needed, taking care of Kelsey, Ian, and the house, and the demands of two sixty-hour-a-week jobs. Sunday nights we'd sit with work calendars, school calendars, and doctor-appointment cards, and we'd hash out possibilities for the week.

"I have clients on Monday," I'd begin, laptop on the table in front of me, so I could get it all down in one place.

Looking down at his leather-bound appointment book, Martin replied, "Okay, I can ask my father to do the job in New Jersey on Monday." Chewing on the end of his pen, he added, "But then I need to leave early on Tuesday morning."

"No problem," I said, inputting Martin's name next to a Monday appointment and moving on to the next scheduling challenge. "Is there any chance you can be back by 4:00? I have a conference call."

We went on like this through the fall, but as the weeks turned into months and new symptoms cropped up, the pursuit of a diagnosis began to span specialties. Appointments became more frequent, and it was painfully clear that we were spreading ourselves way too thin.

Through it all, the voice in the back of my head was still calling. It was ever present, like a splinter or a paper cut: *You need to quit your job.* It wasn't that I couldn't hear it. I wasn't even defying it. It just seemed that following God at a time when financial stability and health insurance were more important than ever was absurd. Martin made good money, but he was an entrepreneur. My job was more stable, and we agreed that now was not the time to rock the boat.

"Through it all, the voice in the back of my head was still calling. You need to quit your job."

It wasn't until years later that I began to see that, as in the days leading to my decision to get sober, I was being prompted to lay down my self-sufficiency, shift my priorities, and learn to trust God and Martin in the face of adversity. I'd spend the early mornings reading about surrender and faith, and go to church on Sunday and sing about it, but this was my son's health we were talking about. This was money and insurance. I believed that following God worked when it came to self-improvement, like getting sober or staying calm in the face of difficulty. But I couldn't be expected to believe that God was actually going to *do* anything about Andrew's health and our finances. Sure, I should pray. But Martin and I needed to keep our oars in the water and steer this family to shore.

That little voice kept nagging at me, though, intensifying through the late fall until, just before Christmas, circumstances made it abundantly clear that I wouldn't be waiting until June to leave my job.

"Joan, I am going to FedEx a package over to the hospital with some background on a proposal that I need you to draft." I was on the telephone with one of my bosses, trying to whisper, since cell phones were not allowed in the hospital room. Andrew was three feet away, watching television with two dozen electrodes glued to his head. We were in a seizure diagnostic center, where I'd stayed overnight with him over the weekend.

The nurses and doctors had been gracious, allowing me to sleep in the bed next to Andrew while we waited for him to faint or exhibit other symptoms so they could examine his brain waves and see if anything was abnormal. We joked that the perpetually flashing light in the patient bathroom wasn't a short circuit but was meant to induce seizures in the patients in order to expedite the process.

"Okay, send it over," I said, totally defeated.

I'd called in to work and told them that I would be out for two or three days, depending on how things played out with Andrew. I was not one to take sick days or to call in sick. On the contrary, I may have been the only woman I know who still missed dinner with the family, even with a work-from-home job. Martin and the kids would be in the kitchen sitting down to eat and I'd be fifteen feet down the short hallway that led to my office, yelling, "I'll be there in a minute" until I'd finally say, "Go ahead without me." Yet another example of my "doing" rather than "being."

As I thought about that FedEx package and the proposal that would come out of it, I started to pray.

God, what is this? I am trying so hard to do the right thing with Andrew. To do the right thing with work. To do the right thing with Martin, Kelsey, and Ian. To do the right thing with you. Why is everything getting so hard?

I can't recall exactly when it happened. It may have been that night, or a few days later. But some time after that night, that prayer, and that FedEx package, something happened in me. It was one of those "Aha!" moments, like the Grinch had with Whoville or Ebenezer Scrooge experienced with the Cratchetts. It was as though a shroud had been lifted, and I was able to see and feel that my priorities were all wrong. Furthermore, despite justifying my work as ultimately serving my family, it became clear that the priorities I'd set actually served my own ego.

Ouch.

I remembered the question I had asked myself when I first felt prompted to leave my job: Who would I be without my job? Now, I began to see it the other way around. Who was I *with* my job? Or, an even better question, Who did I *think* I was with my job? My money? My title? Whether it was that night, sitting on that bed in the dimly lit hospital room with Andrew, or a day or two later, I know that something broke in me; for the first time since it came up in my thinking, I went from *thinking* I was supposed to leave work to *knowing* it.

Interestingly, this knowing did not erase the questions, Who would I be? What would I do? Where would this take me? But the flavor of the questions had changed. Before, these questions tasted like iron or steel. Who would I be? was seasoned with concerns about status and position. Now it was glazed with excitement and wonder: Who *would* I be? I was embarking on an adventure. My hesitation was replaced by eagerness. I wanted to do it and I wanted to do it now.

> "It was as though a shroud had been lifted, and I was able to see and feel that my priorities were all wrong."

"I felt like a human zipper coming undone as God opened me up and showed me the best and the worst of myself."

And yet I still waited, but this time for an entirely different reason. As I contemplated an immediate move, I could see that, in addition to my desire to follow God, part of my do-it-now feeling was motivated by a not so godly desire to tell my bosses where they could stick their FedEx package. The old me was lobbying to put the screws to them, but (un)fortunately, this new me felt that flipping my bosses the bird and walking away without a two-week notice might not be putting my best foot forward. I felt like a human zipper coming undone as God opened me up and showed me the best and the worst of myself through the lens of day-to-day life.

I decided to talk it through with Martin, using him as a sounding board to examine my motives. "I don't think I am supposed to wait until June," I told him, sharing the FedEx story and the mini-epiphany that followed.

"When are you supposed to do it, then?" he asked. I could see that he was concerned, but I could also see that he was ready. My being at home would make his work situation much smoother, since he had been rearranging his schedule to keep a dozen balls in the air as well. He would be better off, the kids would be better off, and I . . . well, I was not sure what it would be like for me, but I was ready to give it a shot.

"I am not sure. I don't want to be reactive, but I also don't want to wait. I think the time is coming, but I don't want to be willful." I paused, trying to sort through my thoughts and answer his question.

Martin waited, giving me the time I needed to turn these thoughts over in my head.

"I think I should keep working until the next time I find myself in one of these FedEx-package situations. This way, I am not choosing the day; God is."

We agreed that, while it was a little like playing rock, paper, scissors with a decade-long career, it made sense when viewed through the lens of my fledgling understanding of this new faith. I prayed daily that everything would fall into place if I was supposed to stay at work while watching for the scheduling conflict that would signal that it was all over. And then finally, later that winter, it happened.

It was a Friday morning, and I was in New York visiting a key client. They had scheduled an event that I would have no choice but to attend. I recognized the date, but had to wait until I got back home to my office to confirm. It was the same day as an appointment with a specialist on Long Island that we had been waiting more than two months to see. Both were critical. Both required my presence. Neither could be rescheduled. There was no juggling this one, and I knew this was it.

I shared the news with Martin later that afternoon. Without turning my head from the computer, where I was typing up my resignation letter, I said in a calm, even tone, "Today's the day." My back was to him as he walked through the door into the office.

"The day for what?" It had been weeks since we'd decided on this method for discerning this decision, so he wasn't expecting it.

Not elated, but not upset, I turned in my swivel office chair and faced him. "Today is *the* day."

With the benefit of my facial expression, which was serious yet resigned, he now knew what I meant.

"Oh. *That day*." He put his hand on the back of his black leather desk chair, rolled it toward me, and sat down. "How do you know?"

I explained the dilemma with the client event and Andrew's meeting with the specialist.

"Well," he said. "I definitely think you are supposed to be at this appointment with Andrew and me. Are you sure you can't miss this thing at work?"

"I could, but it would be the beginning of the end for me."

He thought for a moment before saying, "Okay, then, when are you going to do it?"

"Right now." I told him. "I have the e-mail here, but I want to call and let them know it is coming."

And I did. There were a few conversations with human resources that included halfhearted, polite attempts to get me to stay. But actually, I think they were happy that I decided to go. They were looking for a certain kind of worker in my position, the kind who was always going to put work and clients first. I'd been that kind of worker for the entirety of the four years I worked there, but as I began to change, the woman I was at work also began to change. I was unemployed by choice and had little notion of what was next. And now things at home were about to change as well.

Surrender

I'm not sure what I thought would have happened if I didn't follow God, but when he went from a nice little story to something powerful enough to knock me off my feet and lead me around like a lost puppy, disobedience seemed like a less than intelligent option. I never felt as if I would be punished if I didn't obey. There was never a sense of coercion. But I had been given such a strong and immediate faith that it powered everything I did. By the end of January 2004, I was home, Andrew was being homeschooled by a tutor provided by the school district, and our household income had been cut in half.

The financial state of affairs might sound dramatic until you consider that, in addition to Martin's ample salary, we had woven a significant safety net of savings, retirement accounts, and real-estate investments, including holding substantial equity on our house.

And it was some house. Our dream home. Our "we have arrived" house. While it was no mansion, I'd be lying if I said that it didn't make a statement. The brick façade and a dozen windows looked out over a wide expanse of well-manicured lawn and landscaping that had been professionally installed and was professionally maintained. A lovely cobblestone drive straddled by huge stone columns set the tone for the impression we were trying to create—substantial and elegant. Think *Southern Home* meets *Fine Homebuilding*.

Inside, custom oak floors with walnut inlays supported fine furnishings and impeccable design. Three floors housed formal and informal living space that allowed us to work, relax, and entertain in comfort and style. We were proud of how it looked and even more proud of what it represented.

Aside from just the grandeur of it, building it had been a labor of love. It was 1999 when we first set out to build a house, and we did not have the kind of money we had just a few years later. On the contrary, Martin was just gearing up his business and I was working for a dot-com company that was losing steam as the tech bubble burst. We were up-and-comers. Married since December 1996, we had three children, had career momentum, and had just purchased a desirable piece of land. It was on a cul-de-sac in Warwick, which had changed dramatically since the *New York Times* began featuring it as a hot, rural suburb for artists, writers, and affluent thirty-somethings to consider when they were ready to settle down outside the city. Transitioning from "on our way" to arrival, we created an impressive living space that was one of the last rungs left on the ladder of our success. No strangers to hard work, we were willing to invest some sweat equity in order to get there.

Martin and I were workhorses, and our skills were completely synergistic. Unlike me, Martin was brilliant when it came to details. The building term "measure twice, cut once," was coined for him. The back of his white van was arranged like a fine clothing store. He'd built custom shelves that allowed for maximum use of space. There was a place for everything, from the large-belt sanding machines to the smallest twopenny nail. He was never late, and his work ethic was impeccable. On top of that, he ran his business on a pay-as-you-go basis. If he didn't have the money, he didn't spend it. He was happy when things were steady and predictable.

I, on the other hand, had a dozen "junk drawers" in every house I'd ever owned. Organization, paperwork, anything that had to do with attention to detail was my nemesis. But give me a problem to solve or a vision to cast, and I was your lady. I could see our house built on that land before we had a plan, and I knew we would come up with the money without checking the numbers. Martin would ask the practical questions, and I would assure him that we would have what we needed when we needed it.
And we always did.

Over the course of our short marriage, we had learned that if we made plans and put ourselves behind implementing them, there was nothing that we couldn't do. Whether it was

> *"We had learned that if we made plans and put ourselves behind implementing them, there was nothing that we couldn't do."*

growing a business, building houses, becoming landlords, or subdividing and selling land, we found that, working together, we were a formidable force.

That was how, doing much of the work ourselves, we were able to build a house that was bigger and more beautiful than anything that we could have hoped to afford. We were in lockstep in our desire to make a better life and were willing to break our backs to grab our little piece of the American dream.

If I were to hazard a guess about where this drive to succeed came from, I'd say it was rooted in the fact that Martin and I are both first-generation people of sorts. I'm a first-generation white-collar worker, whose parents had taken chances to make a better life for their children. Leaving Brooklyn with very little money to move to a rural town where they knew no one was not easy for either of them.

My father worked two and three jobs at a time to keep them afloat, which left my mother home alone much of the time with five kids under ten years old to care for. Later, when my father suffered an injury that led to early retirement, my mother went back to school, became a nurse, and, eventually, became a nurse administrator. Hard work, sacrifice, and inge-nuity resulted in their having a very comfortable life, despite the scraping and saving that had been necessary to get there. They had a vision for their lives and a vision for ours. We had been brought up to take up where they had left off, raising life to the next level for ourselves and our children.

Martin was a first-generation American. He and his family,

none of whom spoke English, came from Uruguay in 1985, when he was fifteen. They arrived with one thousand dollars, which they'd borrowed, and little more than the clothes on their backs. He and his family had hopes for a better future, but like many immigrants, did not know what that might actually mean.

I can't tell you how many times I have sat at a table with my mostly happy-go-lucky husband and watched his eyes dim as he described what he had been expecting upon his arrival in the great America, land of opportunity. He'd seen TV sitcoms and dramas back in Uruguay, shows like *Diff'rent Strokes* (which they called Arnold) and *Eight is Enough* (which they called Tender Dad), but it was the movie *E.T.* that had really captured his imagination. He dreamed of the cul-de-sacs and tree-lined streets, BMX bikes and Reese's Pieces. That was what America was for him: an affluent, middle-class existence that would never be possible for him in his homeland.

It was March when Martin's family arrived at JFK Airport in New York. Some old friends from the Montevideo neighborhood picked them up. For all of its economic shortcomings, Montevideo had been a clean and beautiful European-style city. There, while they might have had to share a single-size bottle of Coca-Cola as a treat, the family lived in a small but well-kept apartment. But Martin was expectantly looking for something more.

As they left New York City and began to drive through affluent Westchester County, Martin asked, *"¿Así es donde vivís vos?"* (Does it look like this where you live?)

"No, no espera ya vamos a llegar." (Wait, we'll get there.)

As the car wound through suburban New York into the

more rural suburbs of Orange County, he asked again, *"¿Así es donde vivís vos?"*

"No, no espera ya vamos a llegar."

About an hour later, when they had left the more rural suburbs and turned to park next to a line of full-to-bursting Dumpsters in a small, rundown apartment complex, he did not ask again. He knew that they had arrived at his new home, and it looked nothing like the ones in *E.T.*

Less than a year after they arrived, Martin received a call from his sister while at school. Their mother had been caught up in an INS raid at the factory where she worked. The family needed to move quickly. Just when they had begun to get settled, they were forced to pack whatever they could carry and move in with a friend. The four of them shared one room until they could find another place to go. Martin, still fifteen, traded his soccer ball for a hammer and began working for a hardwood-flooring company. He had never done construction, nor had his father, who had worked as a radio engineer in Uruguay. Martin was paid ten dollars a day and his father twenty a day as they learned the back-breaking trade of laying and finishing hardwood floors. That was when Martin was introduced to the kind of houses that we built together. Houses he never thought he would ever live in.

That's why it stung so much when we had to sell it.

Martin, I think we are supposed to sell the house," I said, rolling over in bed at 2:30 A.M. We had been living there for about three years. Just long enough to be extremely comfortable.

"Sell the house?" he responded, groggy from being woken abruptly.

He was getting used to my waking up in the middle of the night, but this was the first time one of my late-night prayer junkets had included a new directive. Had this happened months earlier, there might have been more dialogue. But it had been nearly a year since my conversion, and we were beginning to accept that my bold "I think we are supposed to . . ." statements were coming from a spiritual place. Letting go was beginning to feel normal in its abnormality.

As the months had passed and I had more and more experiences hearing and following the prompting of the Holy Spirit in my life, I was growing in confidence regarding what it was that I heard. I wasn't cocky. In fact, it was just the opposite. My study had brought me to story after story of arrogant leaders like King Saul, who was an anointed follower of God who had fallen off track to his destruction. I read these stories less as threats and more as warnings. I was no psychic—just a regular person who sensed God was leading her life and who tried her best to follow that lead. If I began making myself out to be anything other than that—to others or in my own mind—I would be in trouble, and I knew it.

As insurance against that pitfall, I had decided that my first response to thinking I was hearing something from God was to assume that I was not. I'd put the thought on the shelf and go about my business until I encoun-

> " 'Martin, I think we are supposed to sell the house,' I said, rolling over in bed at 2:30 A.M."

> *"Letting go was beginning to feel normal in its abnormality."*

tered something outside of my own influence that confirmed it. Sometimes it was an encounter with a person or something on television— anything significant that supported my sense of a guidepost in the right direction. Then, if I felt that the time was right, I would go for it. If I was still unsure, I would wait.

I think this kind of unabashed following was easier for me than it was for Martin, even though he had been a Christian since he was a child. He believed, and believed strongly, in the tenets of the Christian faith, but stepping out to let God have his way with him was new and different. He was willing, but he was generally a little more cautious than I was in taking the next step. Of course, that tracks with our personalities. But I also understand that I was the one feeling compelled to make the changes, not him.

"And where are we supposed to go?" he asked.

"I wish I had a better answer, but I don't know," I replied. "I just know that we are supposed to do it."

While leaving my job had impacted us as a family, it was still a decision I'd made about my life. Selling this house upped the ante. We had no idea why this might make sense or where we were supposed to go from here. Sure, we'd been moving in this direction, but this was the last straw in making *my* spiritual journey into *our* spiritual journey, and Martin needed to think about it.

But it didn't take him long.

Neither of us liked to pray out loud, which made doing it together particularly awkward for both of us. But that night I fell asleep in Martin's arms as he prayed quietly, "God, I am not sure what you are doing or why you would care where we live, but we want to do what you want us to do. Help us to know where you want us, and we will go."

When we woke up several hours later, Martin turned to me and said with a hint of sadness in his voice, "Okay, if you are confident that this is what God is asking us to do, I think we should do it."

———————

Abraham was called by God and asked to leave his home, and go to the land that God had prepared for him, even though he wasn't sure where that was. In faith, he left his home and followed the sound of God's voice. He went without knowing to a place he was not sure of to something he was uncertain about.

I came across Abraham's story for the first time later that week, and I found it both confirming and comforting. He went without knowing, and while he made his share of mistakes and took a few lumps for them, God always stuck with him, and Abraham always listened and always followed. We had no idea where we were going or why we were going there, but our faith was growing stronger, as was our resolve to follow this wherever it took us. We put our house on the market later that same week.

There is more than one way to interpret this move. Maybe we were super-faithful. Then again, maybe we were super-crazy. I'm not sure that either of us was completely sure which it was, but we were confident that we were on some kind of journey and that going back was not an option. In retrospect, Martin tells me that he's not exactly sure why he went along with me so easily—only that he knew that the change in me was radical enough and consistent enough that he believed it was really God at work. As for me, I just kept reading the Bible—praying for wisdom, guidance, and knowledge; looking for confirmation; and being obedient when I felt confident that God was calling.

And really, while we were stepping out in faith, we also had some solid facts to hang our hats on. Our home was beautiful. We *knew* that it would sell in no time and that we could build an equally beautiful (but smaller) house while being faithful to the less-is-more lesson that we thought God was trying to teach us. This was 2004, just about the peak of the biggest housing boom in American history. This was way before the average American knew anything about any worldwide credit crisis or expected that American real estate would do anything but continue its upward trajectory. Sure, we were following the leading of the Holy Spirit, but it didn't hurt to know that houses were flying off the market in a matter of days, often at prices higher than the asking prices because bidding wars would break out.

"There is more than one way to interpret this move. Maybe we were super-faithful. Then again, maybe we were super-crazy."

We had a hot house in a hot market, so the risk of following was worth the potential rewards. We were so sure that the house would sell quickly and for top dollar that we began building the new house before we sold the old one. *No problem*, we thought. *The market is hot, our place is gorgeous. God's got our back. How can we go wrong?*

We were about to learn that pride does, in fact, go before the fall and that God is bigger than the markets—whether they are up or down. To our surprise and the surprise of a host of Realtors and market experts, our wonderful house that made us so very proud did not sell for a year.

At first we remained cool about it. We were doing the right thing. Of course, God would respond quid pro quo and work out the details for us. And didn't we deserve it? Wasn't our radical faith worthy of reward? As the weeks passed and people came to see the house, we were sure that we would get a great offer any day. We did receive one offer about a month into the process for about seventy thousand dollars less than the asking price. We scoffed at it. How could they even think of offering that little for this house? Not only was it beautiful, we had put our hearts and souls into it. The house was our pride and joy, and we wanted top dollar.

Our confidence faded into dread as progress on our new house began to pick up steam. We were rapidly reaching the point at which it would be impossible to close on the first house before we had to take title to the second. Remember, I was not working and the construction business was starting to show early signs of what was to become a substantial recession. By August 2004, when our new house was built and we found ourselves paying two hefty mortgages with half our previous income, we started to get nervous.

Radical faith or no, we were losing everything. As the weeks and months passed, we became increasingly worried. The more worried we got, the more we tried to make a sale

> *"Radical faith or no,
> we were losing everything."*

happen. We reduced the price, made flyers, and tried to be there when the buyers came (a desperate tactic that I would not recommend). It seemed as if the more we tried to make the sale happen, the less action there was on the house.

Something wasn't right. Where was that be-a-good-Christian-and-get-all-the-blessings help the televangelists were always talking about? We weren't supposed to be losing everything that we'd worked so hard to obtain.

One by one, we emptied bank accounts, liquidated insurance policies, and cashed out retirement funds to pay our bills. Our little empire was collapsing, and with no offers and decreased showings on the house, we were on the brink of losing our suburban palace. This Christian experiment appeared to be backfiring.

Then one day while I was journaling at the café and lamenting my misfortune, something clicked. It was the same kind of shroud-raising moment I had experienced when I realized that my work did not define me. As if swept in by a wind of calm understanding, it became clear—we had to let it go. We had to be willing to lose it all, even if it came to foreclosing on our house, moving into a rental apartment, and starting over. God was not just asking us for a *commitment*, we were being called to complete, ego-busting *surrender*.

The pre-conversion Joan had always considered faith to be a crutch, and maybe it was. But I had never once considered that my VP title, six-figure salary, and bigger than necessary house were also crutches—crutches that I had used to bear the weight of my insecurities and my unhealthy need for the approval of others. I began to realize that, despite my illusion of independence, I had always leaned on something. Intellect and reason, drugs and alcohol, money and prestige: they had all been crutches for me. And I was being given a choice: to lean on these things that I could see and touch or to release them and lean on this undefined hope promised by this new faith.

I shared this insight with Martin, but he did not have the same warm, fuzzy peace about the notion of losing everything. He'd already been down that road, and he was not embracing the notion of doing it again.

"Sometimes I think you *want* that to happen," he said through frustration that bordered on anger. He was leaning back, his hands gripping the edge of our ten-thousand-dollar granite countertop.

"No, I don't want it to happen," I curtly responded to his accusing tone. "I wish the house would sell tomorrow, I wish Andrew was getting better, I wish I could have this faith and have a job, but that's not how it is going down."

He looked across the kitchen island to where I was sitting at the wooden table. He was incensed—with me, with himself, maybe even with God. "I know what you are saying is the right thing. I just don't want to go there."

I knew what he meant. We'd both gone through our own versions of losing everything and bouncing back. The thought of having nothing—this time with three kids—was excru-

> *"God was not just asking us for a commitment, we were being called to complete, ego-busting surrender."*

"So, like jumping out of a plane in tandem, we chose to let go."

ciating. But here we were. We could hold on for dear life, cursing God for not doing things our way, or we could accept our lot and trust that everything would be all right.

We bickered on and off like this for a few days, Martin, wondering what we should be doing that we were not yet doing, and me, resigned to the fact that this was out of our hands. And then, one evening after a long day of work, he sat on the couch next to me and said, "We have no choice." He was calm and even. Not emotionless, but serene. "We have to keep going. It makes no sense to argue about this." Finally, the peace that had found me days earlier found Martin as well.

So, like jumping out of a plane in tandem, we chose to let go.

As if God had waved a magic wand, we stopped worrying about the house and the bills. Some combination of surrender, despair, and lack of options converged to allow us to motor on and push through. We decided that if the house we were living in didn't sell, we would put FOR SALE signs on it *and* the new one, and live in whichever one was left. We were prepared to go wherever we were meant to go and (although some days were better than others) to release the outcome.

As if to illustrate the simple Bible passage that tells us to "cease striving and know that I am God," when we finally stopped striving, our dream house sold to a couple from New York City with two children. The deal went through less than two weeks before our coffers were completely empty and we would have been unable to pay our bills. As a result, our sadness about leaving the house we had always dreamed of was balanced by a sense of relief and gratitude for getting just what we needed, just when we needed it. By surrendering the process, we gained a peace and stability that our desire for control had always promised but never delivered.

But apparently, God wasn't done with us yet.

Skydiving in the Nude

That's it, I've had enough." Martin was perched on the edge of the couch with his elbows on his knees, running his hands through his shoulder-length black hair and staring at a half dozen piles of paperwork on the coffee table in front of him. This posture of defeat had become a regular part of his workday for the past four or five months, as a parade of difficult customers had begun to erode his peace of mind and the stability of his hardwood-flooring business.

It was usually not like this for Martin. His company had been built on a foundation of high praise from past clients and word-of-mouth referrals. In more than twenty years of working with both commercial and residential customers, he had never once been a party to a lawsuit. Now, in the space of four months, during the summer of 2006, he'd been named in three.

I looked at him across the wide expanse of our kitchen/ family room, wondering if he was going to let his mounting frustration take hold of him. Martin is a mild-mannered guy 95 percent of the time, but sometimes he'd let the nitpicking details of the latest work drama or a handful of other hot-button issues get under his skin. Then, man, could he blow! I waited to find out whether this would be one of those times.

Over the past month or so, I'd sensed that Martin was on the cusp of a radical change. There was something about the unrelenting and atypical pressure surrounding his work life that reminded me of those last months I had spent in my PR position. I couldn't help but think that, like that day I received that FedEx package at the hospital, something was ready to shift in him. I just had no idea where it might take him.

And the stress at home wasn't helping. Nearly two years after his symptoms had begun and I had left my job, we were no closer to an answer regarding Andrew's health. Some doctors said it was neurological. Others thought it might be hormonal. The truth was, no one knew, and Andrew had missed so much school as a result of his mystery illness that we were being forced to consider a radical, last-resort option: sending him to a boarding school that could both accommodate his medical needs and provide the kind of education a teenager with his intelligence and drive required.

This was something none of us, including Andrew, wanted. We thought he was too young to be away from the stability of home, and he was adamant in his desire to remain close to his family and friends and get back to school. But we were running out of options. It was either boarding school or our bright son, who loved school and aspired to earn a

> *"We were being forced to consider a radical, last-resort option: sending him to a boarding school."*

PhD one day, would be left back a grade, another something none of us wanted.

As the decisions regarding Andrew's school placement came to a head, Martin and I were both feeling the pressure. So when the business that Martin had once loved began to drive him up the wall, it was enough to push him over the edge.

Martin's background as a carpenter was valuable, but it was not highly transferrable. He'd been forced to drop out of school when he went to work at fifteen, and though he'd later gone back to get his GED, starting over in his midthirties with a high-school education and twenty years of construction-industry experience somewhat narrowed his options in the job market. At least, it would have if we had been thinking practically.

But as my experience with God continued in an unrelenting, mysterious way, we were beginning to see that thinking practically was not our only option. Maybe not even our preferred option. In the midst of our turmoil at home, I had continued to follow the voice that had prompted me to pray on the floor of my room and nudged us to sell our dream house. This same voice also prompted me to attend writing conferences in New Mexico and California, and with little effort beyond pulling together a book proposal and showing up, I met some people who embraced me and knew their way around the Christian publishing industry.

As with so many of the connections and contacts I

"We were beginning to see that thinking practically was not our only option."

made then and afterward, I had no idea until later that these people had considerable influence. My new contacts included the literary agent who eventually took me on as his client, the acquisitions editor who eventually acquired this book, and a magazine editor who was the first to pay me for my writing. Martin and I both knew that, given my background and lifelong aversion for this faith, I barely had any business being a Christian, let alone becoming a Christian writer. So it was easy to see that unimaginable (and unlikely) doors were opening for me even as things at home were becoming more and more challenging. I wasn't sure where any of this was taking me, but I remained committed to moving forward and letting go. With a peace of mind that defied my understanding and predisposition, I just kept following.

Martin's journey wasn't working out quite the same way. When he faced a decision or turning point, I would ask him, "What do you hear? What is God telling you?"

"Nothing," he would reply. "I don't hear anything. God doesn't talk to me like he talks to you."

"I don't believe that," I would tell him. "You're just not listening."

This would inevitably lead to an argument—him, annoyed that I was "preaching" to him, and me, annoyed that he was not seeking God deeply enough. We'd go around and around like that until any chance of getting anywhere had vanished in a fog of mutual recriminations. Looking over at Martin from the kitchen that day, I was determined not to go down that path again.

When work got the better of Martin, the last thing he wanted was a pep talk or a "Get over it, you big baby" lecture. Offering statements like, "Just try to let it go, honey" or "Why do you let them get to you?" led to what you might expect: him furious and me convinced that he was beyond assistance.

He'd told me before, in the postargument calm, that when his frustration mounted, he was simply looking to vent. I was supposed to skip the attempts at problem solving and avoid preaching. There's nothing like a self-righteous Christian know-it-all to make you want to blow your brains out when you're hurting. But by God's grace, that evening I did it differently. Rather than offer a list of prayers or suggestions about how he could apply spiritual principles to *fix* it or immediately *accept* it, I just waited quietly, anticipating the now familiar monologue that I knew would come next.

"HGTV has killed the construction industry."

Here we go. I hate to admit it, but I wanted to laugh. Not out of a lack of compassion, but because this particular rant, which I had heard a dozen times before, was hysterical. In fact, it was one of my favorites.

"These freaking people don't even know how to pick up a hammer, and they watch two episodes of *Weekend Warrior* and suddenly they're flooring experts."

Oh Lord, help me to keep a straight face.

Martin is that guy at a party who effortlessly finds himself in the middle of a circle of strangers, telling stories, playing music, and making people laugh. They might be laughing at him or with him, but he's perfectly content either way. Unlike me, Martin is rarely serious, even when he is actually *trying* to be. This made it all the more difficult to pretend to commiserate when he slid off the couch onto the floor and began to deliver his impressions.

First, he took on the role of the picky customer, scanning the floor on bended knee looking for bubbles or dust in the finish. "I know I left the dogs out while you were working when you asked me not to, but I can see one dog hair right here."

Then, jumping to his feet in one swift motion, he changed his voice and became an evil-twin version of himself, the contractor whose work was being maligned. This retaliatory monologue was a stream of colorful epithets fit for mature audiences only.

In reality, Martin would never speak to a customer that way. Unfortunately, despite his spot-on comedic timing and impeccably executed pratfalls, I knew that the frustration he was feeling was real.

"I know, honey," I finally interrupted, feigning seriousness and biting my lip to keep from laughing. "Maybe it is time to close the business."

This wasn't the first time we'd discussed this option. More than twenty years of flooring was taking its toll on his back and knees. His hands were tightening up, resulting in lost dexterity when he played guitar, which was where his true passion lay. But Martin's exhaustion was more than physical. He was tired of running his own business. He was tired of fighting the elements and fighting the customers and having to scrap for new jobs against fly-by-night operations that had sprouted up in the wake of the post-2000 real-estate bubble.

He'd come a long way since his humble arrival in the United States; he no longer saw the country as a magical *E.T.* kingdom, and yet he was beginning to get the itch to pursue some dreams of his own. Just as time away from my work

> *"Martin's exhaustion was more than physical. He was tired of running his own business."*

had given me the freedom to examine my life choices, he was beginning to consider life beyond floors. But he was still a long way from accepting that his newly invigorated interest in his own faith and some unlikely door openings might just be the workings of the Holy Spirit in his life.

I couldn't blame him, really. I mean, crazy as it sounds, I was actually beginning to believe that I was called out of PR to be a writer. It may have seemed a little reckless at the time, but it was not that much of a stretch. After all, I'd made a good chunk of my living drafting press releases and media kits, practicing the art of reducing complicated concepts to simple sentences. It wasn't bad training. As bold as it sounds to imagine one might get inside God's head (if God even has a head), I could see the spiritual logic in my career shift. But Martin was getting hit with the urge to pursue something about as far from his vocation as it was possible to get.

———————

Three or four months before Martin's HGTV-bashing meltdown on the couch, we'd taken our youngest son to an audition for a local community-theater production of *Joseph and the Amazing Technicolor Dreamcoat*. It was a new community-theater company, and this was to be their first performance. Our then eight-year-old son, a flaming redhead with an over-the-top Broadway personality, took command of the small audition space from the moment he walked in the door.

"Hi, I'm Ian," he said to the director as he grabbed a pencil and application form from the small table in the entryway of a twenty-square-foot room. Ever the budding professional, he filled out his paperwork, sang a rousing version of a Disney song and secured a part on the spot. No need for stage parenting for Ian, who had been singing, dancing, and hamming it up since he was three years old. Thrilled that the process had gone so successfully and quickly, Martin and I were discussing where we might grab a bite to eat when the producer called out to Martin, "Excuse me, do you sing?"

The question caught him off guard. He turned his head, but kept walking to the door as he replied sheepishly, "Well, yeah. But not *this* stuff." Martin had revealed his distaste for musicals early in our marriage by responding with a single word, "Boooooooring," whenever I suggested we catch a Broadway show.

Not put off by Martin's poorly veiled disgust, the producer continued: "Well, you have the perfect look for one of the lead characters. Why don't you sing something for us and let us decide."

"I can't," he told the director. "I'm not an actor. I mean, What would I sing?"

"Oh, come on," I said, half-teasing and half-thinking about how nice it would be for Ian and Martin to do something together.

Cajoling Martin rarely worked when his mind was made up, but he could be pushed if he was on the fence. I gave it a shot. "What do you have to lose, Babe? Just sing anything."

The director chimed in. "It doesn't matter what song you choose as long as we can get a feel for your range and tone."

Martin looked at me as if I might rescue him. No such luck.

"Sing anything, Daddy," Ian added in. *We've got him now,* I thought. With all that had been happening with Andrew's illness over the past two years, Ian had at times gotten lost in the shuffle. While he never showed it, all the turmoil had to have been hard on him. This would be a perfect opportunity for them to share some father-son bonding time. I could tell by the look on Martin's face that he was ready to give in.

His voice betrayed a hint of nervousness as he turned to me and asked me, "What should I sing?"

"I don't know," I said, trying to think of a song that would play well in an audition and for which he would re-member the lyrics. "How about 'Blue Sky'?"

For as long as I'd known him, Martin had been a singer-songwriter who played guitar and piano. He is one of the few people I'd ever met who feels no shame in announcing his love for eighties hair bands, Southern rock, and Spanish ballads, and yet still manages to come across as more cool than cheesy—most of the time. I'd both watched him perform and per-formed with him on numerous occasions over the years, but I'd never before or since enjoyed a performance like this one.

He stood in the center of the room still obviously a little nervous. Looking over at me for one last out, he turned and sang a spot-on version of the Allman Brothers' "Blue Sky" that would have made Gregg Allman and Dickey Betts proud.

I don't think either of us had ever made the "Lord" con-nection in that song, which we had sung at open mics dozens of times before that moment. After he finished, they asked if he could sing it up an octave. And he did. Then up another octave. And he did. I always loved to hear Martin sing, but I'd never had the opportunity to hear him test what turned out to be an impressively wide range. We actually walked out the door with him playing a lead as the Frenchman brother of Joseph, named Ruben.

Community theater in suburban New York is not Broad-way, but it was enough to give him a taste of the stage and prompt him to learn that he loved it. From the rehearsals to the performance, and everything in between, he was enamored with the theater. Even the chores, like moving and packing sets, got him excited. This passion for performing had welled up out of nowhere and could not be contained. After *Joseph* he got a part in *Oliver!* with the same company. He subscribed to *Back Stage*, an actors' Web site and magazine that included lists of audition opportunities in the tristate area and beyond. In less than six months he landed his first paid role as Joseph of Arimathea in a long-running production of the *The Passion Play*. Next came some children's theater opportunities in Pennsylvania, which suited him well since, as the HGTV *Weekend Warrior* skit in our living room demonstrated, Martin has a natural talent for physical comedy, which kids love.

It appeared that, in the same way as I found myself a budding and unlikely author, Martin had developed a new vocation. But balancing his acting—soon more of a part-time job than a hobby—with his business was tearing him apart. I could see, having endured a similar process of reorientation two years earlier, that he was approaching a choice.

This was not a simple matter, though. It wasn't just about choosing between acting and his business, any more than mine had been a choice between PR and writing in 2004. Instead, he was facing the choice of operating within the illusion of control and certainty that appeared to reside in his business or stepping out into an unknown and un-

> *"This passion for performing had welled up out of nowhere and could not be contained."*

likely future. Talk about a test. It is hard enough to let-go-and-let-God when it comes to work and finances, but *acting*? Could God have picked a less practical and less financially secure profession to throw Martin's way? While my choice to step out in faith and leave my career had required some courage, Martin faced a choice that was downright irrational. There was no other income to rely on. No company to create a benefits package. If I had jumped out of the plane with a parachute, he was skydiving in the nude.

After his HGTV rant, Martin settled down and was staring silently out the back window of our family room, past the snow-covered deck into a swell of trees that lined a small pond in the distance. "Maybe I should," he said quietly without turning. I couldn't believe my ears.

I said nothing. Martin had supported my wacky journey every step of the way, which was in itself a variation on stepping out in faith. The difference was that, while we'd taken the risks together, he had been stepping out in *my* faith. He believed that God was doing amazing things in my life, but somewhere deep inside, he did not believe that God would do the same for him. After all of those years of dutifully believing, he'd never really lived as if God was guiding his path. In fact, he was skeptical that he would ever be the one who would receive that kind of grace.

I stood quietly watching him as he wrestled with himself. I prayed without speaking, *God, please help him to do it. Help him to give in and go for it.* It was not lost on me that I was, in effect, praying for financial instability. But I was more interested that Martin, after all of these years of hard work and sacrifice, might finally pursue something for which he felt some genuine passion.

I didn't know if Martin was really supposed to be an actor, any more than I knew whether I was really supposed to be a writer. What I did know—or sensed from the core of my being—was that we were being invited to choose a different path. To let go of certainty and follow without knowing where we would land. I'd been at it since that day in 2003, and while on the surface things appeared to be falling apart, I had never felt more alive, free, or comfortable in my skin as I had since embarking on this adventure.

Martin was along for the ride, but I sometimes felt as if I were a step ahead of him on the road. That was not what I wanted. And given that the first scripture I'd ever encountered talked about the reciprocity of marriage, I didn't think it was how God would have wanted it, either. We were a team. I was convinced that walking shoulder to shoulder, side by side into this had been the plan all along.

Finally, he spoke in a calm, measured way: "I know it makes no sense, but I really think that I am supposed to pursue this acting thing."

There is a certain, familiar look that comes across the face of someone who finally realizes that he has to change. Addicts get it the first time they sincerely agree to go to rehab or attend a recovery meeting. Kids get it when they give up fighting and do what their parents tell them to do. Martin had that kind of look. After years of faithfully believing in God and

> *"While on the surface things appeared to be falling apart, I had never felt more alive, free, or comfortable in my skin."*

following the rules as he understood them, he was working through a different kind of conversion. In that moment, with less force and less fanfare than my experience, his dutiful, long-held, unquestioning belief in the things that God *said* transitioned into a radical faith in what God might actually *do*. He made the leap from supporting what I perceived to be the leading of the Holy Spirit in my life to following God's leading in his own life. He believed in what God could and would do if he were sought with abandon and followed beyond practicality.

Now we were really in for it.

The Wave and the Undertow

He is not breathing."

It was June 2005, and Martin was on his knees on the front seat of the car, leaning over the headrest looking at Andrew, who was upright in the backseat. I wanted to see what was happening, but knew that it would be impossible for me to keep driving seventy miles an hour and look in the backseat without killing the three of us.

"Try it again," I said firmly, trying to maintain my composure.

Martin shifted his weight and gave Andrew a solid poke in the sternum. This instinctual tactic had unnerved me when he'd done it a few minutes earlier, but it had resulted in Andrew taking a big gulp of air and resuming breathing, so I was not going to complain.

I did my best to keep the car on the road as I watched them through the rearview mirror and called out, "Andrew! Wake up, baby! Breathe!"

I'm not sure why I told him to wake up, since his eyes were wide open and he was sitting straight up in the seat. But behind the wheel of our black SUV, driving at breakneck speed in an attempt to cut ten minutes off the fifty-minute drive to Andrew's regular hospital, I was not worried about semantics. I just wanted him to snap out of it.

"What's happening?" I said to Martin in an urgent but measured tone.

"It's not working," he said as he put his face directly in front of Andrew's and yelled. "Breathe!"

Three minutes, three minutes. I wasn't sure, but I recalled hearing somewhere that you couldn't go more than three minutes without oxygen before you experienced brain damage.

"We're not going to make it to Westchester," I said as I slowed the car to make an incredibly dangerous, faster than prudent U-turn at the top of Mount Peter, where I had grown up. I'd hoped to get him to the doctors who were more familiar with his case. This stalled breathing was a new symptom, and I wanted them to see it firsthand. But the sternum thing was not working, and we needed to get him in front of a doctor, any doctor, right now.

I've only driven one hundred miles an hour once before, and that was on the autobahn in Germany, in a BMW that was made for those kinds of speeds. I saw the speedometer climbing as we careened down the incline that led back into Warwick, where there was a small community hospital. I tapped the brake, and my crisis brain kicked in.

Slow down. An accident will just make things worse.

I looked in the rearview mirror and saw Martin, still trying to rouse a breath out of Andrew.

Okay. What is the fastest way to get this six-foot-tall kid out of the backseat of this car and into the hospital? I asked myself, trying to anticipate next steps. *Construction. The hospital has been under construction. Which entrance is best?* I ignored the thirty-mile-per-hour speed limit as we entered the village. *If the*

> *"I saw the speedometer climbing as we careened down the incline that led back into Warwick."*

police try to pull me over, I'll just keep driving. The officers can help us lift him out of the car. I rolled through two stop signs and a red light, and turned into the hospital parking lot before remembering to pray. *God, please help my son. Help him.*

We turned into the parking lot and drove up to the emergency entrance. As if they were waiting there to help, eight huge men stood in a circle, talking, right outside the automatic door.

Yes, God. Thank you.

I learned later that they were all EMTs, waiting for casualties from an accident on the other side of town, but for me they were literally a godsend. I parked the car, jumped out, and starting yelling to them.

"Please help us! My son is not breathing!"

Martin was already in the back with Andrew, trying to get some leverage in an effort to drag 165 pounds of dead weight across the seat and out the door. Within seconds the EMTs were on either side of him, rolling him onto a stretcher that seemed to appear from nowhere.

Okay, Joan, park the car, I said out loud to myself. Martin had gone in with Andrew, and I was standing with the keys in my hand, looking at all four open car doors, trying to get my bearings. *Park the car and go inside.*

"How much more would our lives have to unravel before we could catch a break?"

When I ran in the door, I expected a scene from a medical drama: a team of people working on Andrew, pumping his heart, doing mouth-to-mouth, and hooking him up to machines. What I saw was completely different. Not only was Andrew breathing, he was talking to Martin and asking if he could have something to eat. I was both filled with relief and yet, at another level, not surprised at all to see his rapid recovery. This sort of thing had happened before. Andrew's symptoms were a moving target, as were their repair. The doctors would treat each new symptom as it arose, order more tests, prescribe medicine to see if it had an impact, and then Andrew would get back to "normal," sometimes rapidly, other times more slowly, until something else happened.

And nobody wanted to get back to normal more than Andrew. He was not the kind of kid who enjoyed missing school. He wanted to get back to his friends and his social life and his studies, but the unpredictability of his symptoms made that impossible.

How could this be? I wondered, standing across the ER from Martin and Andrew watching them talk. *How much more would our lives have to unravel before we could catch a break?*

I spent a lot of time in those days reading from the Book of Job. He's the guy in the Old Testament whom God gave over to Satan, confident that he'd stay faithful no matter what

Satan dished out. Job lost everything: his kids, his health, his stature, his friends. But no matter how tough it got or how confused he became about why God would allow these things to happen to him, he remained true to his faith.

Had I read the story of Job before the moment of my conversion, I would have had a million valid, logical questions, like: If Job were so faithful, why would God give him over to Satan instead of just squashing Satan like a bug and being finished with evil once and for all? For that matter, why allow anyone to suffer sickness? Or pain? Or poverty?

And why stop at Job? If preconversion Joan could have talked to this God of the Bible, she would have asked why he had chosen to allow Andrew to be sick. Why did he allow sickness at all?

This made me think about my parents, both in their mid-sixties, who had been battered by illness after illness in the same three-year period. My father had endured treatment and surgery for lung cancer and undergone open-heart surgery, and my mother, kidney cancer and abdominal surgery. Both had been hospitalized for life-threatening infections and other maladies. Is this what God's love looked like?

Not only that, but if this God who loved me so much and called Job faithful was really the big kahuna, why had we been called into financial instability?

None of this made any sense. It wasn't fair.

But then, in the midst of all the turmoil, I sat one morning drinking yet another cappuccino while I squeezed in an hour of read-

"None of this made any sense. It wasn't fair."

ing, writing, and prayer before meeting with the school district to discuss options for Andrew. As I wrote in my journal and contemplated these questions, something dawned on me.

It came on slowly at first, like the word that is on the tip of your tongue or the sneeze that is *right there* but won't quite come. Rather than try to force it, I continued to write and wonder why it was that God had apparently come into my life just to ruin it. All that "God is good" rhetoric didn't seem to apply to my journey at all.

But then some different questions began to surface.

If I planned to hold God's feet to the fire about the things in my life that I perceived to be unfair, wasn't I opening up a Pandora's box? I mean, for fair to be, well, fair, didn't it need to be a two-way street?

I took a sip of coffee and stared at the wall for a minute or two, quietly pondering the notion of "fair" when a follow-up question came to mind. If I deserved better than financial hardship and my family deserved to be healthy and happy, what else did I deserve?

It was like being on one of those spinning rides that hold you on the wall with centrifical force before the floor drops out from under your feet. In an instant, my mind shifted to a whole new class of "whys." For instance, why, after all of those nights that I drove drunk or mixed and matched enough chemicals to throw a person twice my weight into a coma, did I make it home safely without being arrested or having killed myself or some innocent bystander? Or why, in 1993, did Doug, who barely knew me and who had never seen a sip of alcohol pass my lips, decide to hire me for a job that I was marginally qualified for, with no reason or explanation other than that he felt compelled to help me?

As I pondered these "whys," a "what" question came to

mind that has helped shape my understanding of Christianity ever since: What would my life look like if I actually got what I deserved?

I tallied things up: a DWI for every time I drove drunk, an arrest for every time I broke the law, a rep-

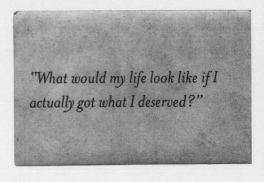

"What would my life look like if I actually got what I deserved?"

rimand for every petulant action and thought. I began to see that "fair" might be a little more than I'd bargained for. Sure, I was game for a God who would help me to get sober and bring peace and prosperity into my life. But did I want to go tit for tat and compare notes on what I owed God compared to what he owed me?

Which brought me back to Job. As I read his story and lived my own, I began to see that there might be something much bigger at play here. Bigger than what career I did or did not have. Bigger than my writing or Martin's acting. Bigger than how much money I had or did not have. Job was rich, then poor, then rich again. God had his own reasons for allowing Job's world to be turned upside down. Maybe the same was true for us. Maybe we were being taken through our paces for a reason. Just because I couldn't imagine what it might be didn't mean it wasn't there.

We were trying our best to do exactly what God wanted us to do. From the jobs to the house to realigning our priorities around church and trying to help other people, we were doing our best to walk the walk and talk the talk, as they say. Yet, it seemed like the more we tried to follow God and do what we perceived we were supposed to do, the more difficult and unpredictable things became.

Sure, we were feeling some peace in the midst of it. But I had to guess that we would have felt even more peaceful if Andrew were healthy and didn't have to go to boarding school. Or if my parents, who lived less than two miles from us, were healthy and enjoyed the retirement they had worked so hard to prepare for. I had no idea why we faced the things that we faced, but I began to see that we needed to play the hand we had been dealt.

We'd chosen to follow this new way of life and do the things we were feeling called to do, and we had to deal with the consequences of that, good or bad. God hadn't put a gun to our heads. He called, and we chose to answer. Through all of this contemplation, I was beginning to see that the moments of peace and the difficulty and trials were not separate from one another.

———————

I'm starting to feel like we are being thrown around in the surf," I said to a friend, having shared with her the latest challenges Martin and I were facing. Linda was one of the people who I had seen for years around town, but never connected with before my shift of faith led me into a new way of dealing with people. One that actually involved *dealing* with people. Since then, we had met frequently for coffee at one of our favorite cafés, usually by chance rather than by appointment. Whether we met at the Tuscan, the Carriage Path, Le Petit Cuisine, or Charlotte's Tea Room (Warwick may be the small-town café capital of the world), our conversations about art, creativity, and letting go informed both of our spiritual journeys, even though we held radically different views on faith.

For some reason, talking with her about the things that God was doing in my life always resulted in a new layer of clarity or insight. A modern-dance choreographer and teacher who had studied at Bard, she had a creative viewpoint that

"She challenged my understanding of this new faith, since she was a Buddhist–leaning cultural Jew with little interest in Christianity."

challenged my business-oriented linear thinking style. She also challenged my processing and understanding of this new faith, since she was a Buddhist-leaning cultural Jew with little interest in Christianity.

I put my elbow on the table and rested my head in my one hand, stirring my now-cold cappuccino listlessly with the other. "These past three years have been both the worst and the best three years of my entire life," I told her. "I can feel myself growing and changing and becoming more peaceful. More interested in other people than I am in myself. And yet, the people I love are suffering, and we are losing everything. The dissonance is hard to bear. It's like I am in this cycle. There's a wave of something wonderful, and I ride it to the crest, only to be dropped down and pulled beneath it by the undertow."

Since I was not much of a beachgoer, owing to a combination of fear (what's *really* swimming around under all that water?) and a frightening lack of melanin that makes me the whitest person on the beach, my only understanding of the concept of undertow was the warnings I got as a kid when my family made the trek across the Marine Park Bridge in Brooklyn to Breezy Point. "Watch out for the undertow," my aunt would say. "It will pull you right under."

This warning may have been the equivalent of the "You can't go in the water until an hour after you eat" ruse that gave adults hope that we might take a short nap during the hottest part of the day, and I don't recall anyone ever getting pulled out to sea, but the image stayed with me. In my elementary-school-aged mind, the waves and the undertow were like an ocean-sized washing machine where the water rose in a beautiful arc toward the sun and the sky, only to crash on the beach, before spitting you back up atop the next wave.

While I'm guessing that the oceanographic accuracy of this description is sorely lacking, this remains the best metaphor I can think of for the challenges of a life lived in faith and the corresponding joys and blessings that come with it.

For some reason that I may never know, it seemed that, for Martin and me—and maybe for everyone—the blessings and challenges of living a life of faith were interwoven and inseparable. What's more, the deeper we went in pursuit of practicing this faith in our day-to-day lives, the more treacherous this undertow became. This was a far cry from the "get Jesus, send some money, and reap the rewards" messages I'd heard on Christian TV.

Don't get me wrong. I don't fault those TV guys. They were some of the first voices I encountered when I was new to this faith, and I learned a lot about God's love and provision from them. But as Martin's and my journey continued, we began to see another side of Jesus' teachings manifested

> *"The deeper we went in pursuit of this faith, the more treacherous these challenges became."*

in our lives—the side that forced us to cry out for mercy in the midst of gratitude.

The wave and the undertow image that we'd discussed that morning never left Linda and me. In fact, she met me a week or two later and handed me a gift. It was a charm bracelet she'd made from Scrabble tiles that spelled out the word *W-A-V-E*. On the flip side of the letters, she wrote a short poem that encapsulated our conversation:

> *keep walking*
> *pushing gently forward*
> *lifting your skirt*
> *letting the undertow pass*
> *again*

Jesus is no genie in a lamp. All the happy thoughts and positive thinking in the world will not keep life from being life. I've come to believe that, as big risks offer the potential for great reward or great failure, the biggest waves bring the swiftest undertow. As I learned to accept this principle rather than fight it, a deeper understanding of the call to *perseverance*, which appears so frequently in the Bible, emerged. As I learned to persevere, something mysterious began to happen: the more difficult things became, the deeper I looked at myself, sought God's guidance, and let go. It is like the scripture that reads, "And not only this, but we also exult in our tribulations, knowing that tribulation brings about perseverance; and perseverance, proven character; and proven character, hope; and hope does not disappoint, because the love of God has been poured out within our hearts through the Holy Spirit who was given to us."

It's not that I think these difficult things happen just to teach us a lesson, any more than I would choreograph difficulties for my children in order to teach them a life lesson. But, I could look back and see that some of the most significant moments of growth, change, and transformation I've experienced were born in times of challenge and difficulty. This leaves me with a choice: I can fight the natural order of things, crying "Why God? Why?" or I can learn to go with the flow.

Dazed and Accused

Joan, I need you to meet with me and the elders next week," Pastor Thomas said in a curt tone that contradicted his normally jovial character. Martin and I had just finished leading worship for a dozen or more attendees of a weeknight discipleship program, and I was saying goodnight for both of us while Martin carried his guitar out to the car.

"What? For what?" I didn't even know who the elders were, not to mention why I might need to meet with them. I looked at him quizzically as I attempted to process the statement through a daze of mental and physical exhaustion. Martin and I had dropped Andrew at boarding school for the first time several hours earlier, which had been devastating for all three of us. We were tired and had toyed with the notion of canceling, but somehow calling in sick to worship just didn't feel right.

"Well," Pastor Thomas proceeded cautiously. "There have been some accusations against you, and we need to discuss them in the presence of the elders."

Accusations? I thought. *What is he talking about?*

It was 2006, and I'd been doing the Christianity thing for just over three years. Having had a few profound insights and weathered a few major storms, I was beginning to think I had the Christian life all figured out. It was simple, really. Just remove the things that got between me and God, listen for his voice, do what he says, persevere through hardship, and, pronto, my path would be straight as an arrow. Sure, I'd need to learn to live with a little uncertainty, since I had absolutely no idea where following Jesus might lead, but as Martin continued with his acting and more doors began to open for my writing, much of the uncertainty seemed more adventure than burden.

As the months had turned to years since my conversion, my ability to trust God deepened, and my world-weary inner skeptic began to soften, allowing me to let my guard down and become part of an increasingly active church community. This new church family had made it easier to navigate Andrew's health issues and endure our less than secure finances. We were learning to find peace in the tension between life's daily challenges and the hope promised by our new faith.

Of course, it didn't happen all at once.

"I was beginning to think I had the Christian life all figured out."

Self-protection by bravado is a hard habit to break. Yet, as I continued to pursue a deeper understanding of the call to love God and my neighbors, the somewhat off-putting demeanor that I'd perfected as a tool to keep people at arm's length slowly began to fade. The more I trusted God, the more I made time for friendships. As a result, Martin and I became close with a few couples, some from church and others we'd met elsewhere, that we hung out with on a regular basis. For the first time in my adult life, I found myself with more than one female friend. We even had people praying for us, which was weird, but nice.

As these relationships began to blossom, I was amazed as a more vulnerable Joan emerged from behind the wall of protection I had, both consciously and unconsciously, constructed to keep myself safe. After all those years of relying on myself, my jobs, my houses, and my things for comfort, I allowed myself to relax a little and rely on the church and other people in a way that I had begun to do in recovery, but never to this extent.

For me this was a radical shift.

I'd always had a love-hate relationship with people. I loved them when they were doing things my way and hated them (or was at least annoyed by them) when they weren't. Whether dealing in business and politics or with friends and family, I was either with you or against you. If I was with you, you could count on me to be rabidly loyal, work until I dropped, and give you the shirt off my back. If I was against you, I might just cut you off and never look back. Unfortunately, Jesus appeared to frown upon such extremes.

Yet as I continued to move forward at God's leading, I was becoming more approachable. People who had never met me before the conversion made off-handed comments about what a friendly

> *"The somewhat off-putting demeanor that I'd perfected as a tool to keep people at arm's length slowly began to fade."*

> "I was part of the team. Or so I thought until I was accused of threatening to kill Pastor Thomas's wife."

person I was. *Friendly? No one had ever in my life described me as friendly.* Helpful? Yes. Intense? Always. Reliable? Absolutely. But friendly? I could count on one hand the number of times someone had chosen that particular adjective to describe me.

Each time I got this kind of feedback, it appeared to be another confirmation that this transformation was real, and I was making true progress. I was now part of the *real* church, the one brimming with nothing but the unconditional love of Jesus and I was part of the team.

Or so I thought, until I was accused of threatening to kill Pastor Thomas's wife.

I wish I could stop here and tell you that this was a joke or that I was just writing it in to see if you were still paying attention, but no such luck. This was real, and it couldn't have come at a time that our family needed the support of the church more.

The morning I was hit with the accusation, Martin and I had driven Andrew to his new school and left him in the care of a team of teachers, doctors, and specialists that we trusted by reputation but did not yet know. He had looked at me with a mix of sadness and anger, as he turned and silently walked away with one of the students who'd been assigned to show him to his room. His protests had been leveled in the weeks leading up to the decision, and he had no fight left. It was heartbreaking.

I was able to hold my tears in long enough to get into the car and close the door. Knowing we were doing the right thing for him didn't mean I was immune to sadness. Martin and I drove up the winding driveway and away from the enormous English Tudor building in silence, his hand on my knee to let me know he was there to talk when I was ready. All I wanted to do was go home and hibernate.

Unfortunately, we had a stop to make first. Having underestimated the emotional kick in the stomach that dropping Andrew off at school would be, Martin and I hadn't thought to find replacements to play a couple of songs for a program at the church that evening. Kelsey and Ian wouldn't be dropped off at home by my in-laws until 8:00 P.M., so we'd have just enough time to knock off the two songs and meet them there.

When we arrived at the church there was no one in the fellowship hall, the main meeting room of the church located on the opposite side of the two-story cinder-block addition where I'd been meeting with Pastor Thomas weekly. We were familiar with the space, since this was where our less formal church service met.

Most of the music equipment was still set up from Sunday morning, so Martin and I busied ourselves with connecting instruments and microphones. We were able to set up in silence, which felt like a blessing at the time. We didn't even feel like talking to each other, not to mention making small talk with the people who were there for the meeting. By the time people started to wander in, we were tuning and doing a sound check, which allowed us to keep to ourselves.

Playing music at a church is a strange and lovely thing for me. It is not like playing a regular song any more than reading the Bible is like reading a regular book. Connected by

> *"There is nothing so sweet as having a genuine experience with God in the midst of sharing a song with people of faith. It can be electric."*

faith and inspired by the Holy Spirit, both experiences are enriched somehow. It's like the difference between watching a romantic movie home alone on the couch and watching the same movie out on a date with a new girlfriend or boyfriend. The date-movie experience sparks an extra something that makes the movie more than a movie. The same goes for singing in a church setting. There is nothing so sweet as having a genuine experience with God in the midst of sharing a song with people of faith. It can be electric.

That evening, in the depth of our sadness over Andrew, we sang two common church tunes, one a contemporary worship song and the other a traditional hymn. The lyrics were simple. First, we sang the hymn:

> *All to Jesus I surrender*
> *All to him I freely give . . .*

And then the more contemporary ballad:

> *Jesus you are, you are.*
> *Everything I'm not*
> *Everything that I'd like to be . . .*

There were more verses that spoke of faith, hope, love, and surrender. Singing them with the dozen or so meeting attendees was simple and intimate, and like the smell of lilacs on a spring morning, that increasingly familiar peace washed over me. I knew that everything would be all right. Andrew would be okay. We would be okay. God was real and in control, even though things were not as we might want them to be. It was a beautiful moment for me, one that I will always remember as bittersweet, given what happened next.

We finished before we knew it, and after packing up his guitar, Martin went out to put it in the car. I hadn't played bass that night, so we were poised to run out quickly. I told him I would meet him out there, and I walked over to say good-bye to Pastor Thomas and confirm our next weekly appointment. That's when he confirmed the accusation.

"You have been accused of threatening a member of the church, and we need to discuss it."

Threatening a member of the church? We'd spent the past three years up to our neck in illnesses, financial challenges, and rending ourselves from the foundation of one life to establish another one. There had been times when I drove from hospital to hospital, visiting Andrew in one and my mother or father in the other. Add to that the quest to find a diagnosis and a school for Andrew; keeping up with Kelsey and Ian and their schools and activities; my studying and writing; and Martin's burning the candle at both ends with his business and acting. Even if I'd had the notion, I didn't have the *time* to threaten anyone.

Unfortunately, my filter was not working well and I could feel the cursing, take-names preconversion Joan bubble to the surface with a fury, propelled by confusion, betrayal, and astonishment. "How dare you?" I said a little too loudly, with a slight waver in my voice that hinted at the potential for a meltdown. This was way too much for me to handle, especially that day. "You knew that we just dropped Andrew off at boarding school. And we come here to fulfill our commitment to this church on the way home, and you're going to hit me with this crap?" I was incensed both at his insensitivity and my cursing.

Martin walked in, perplexed, and asked what was happening. He knew my look and that tone, and that he needed to get me out of there before things got even uglier. I turned away without another word, and filled Martin in on the ride home.

"Can you believe this?" I was furious. Every bit of the peace and trust and warmth I had been feeling about the church and this new journey with God was shattered by what felt like an irreparable betrayal, delivered at a moment of maximum vulnerability. How could this be happening?

"Who could I possibly have threatened?" I was racking my brain to figure out what the pastor might possibly have been referring to. "We are at this freaking church three times a week, working our tails off, trying to spend time with our kids and support this place, and this is how they're going to repay us?" Martin remained quiet. He knew that, like the day he had needed to vent about the HGTV clients, I needed to get this out before I would be able to have a rational conversation about the events of the day.

By the time we got home I was all yelled out. Between Andrew and the mystery accusation, I had nothing left. We changed, sat down on the couch, and agreed that we needed to forget it. I had not threatened anyone about anything. No one in their right mind was going to believe that I had. We couldn't imagine why this had happened, but we convinced ourselves that this must be some kind of misunderstanding that would be remedied quickly, and then we would get back to our comfortable little church groove.

No such luck.

I was informed the next day that I had been accused by the pastor's wife of threatening to murder her, with the intention of divorcing Martin and marrying her husband. Martin and I went to Pastor Thomas's office to receive the news, but the details were sketchy, and when we pressed him, he was not forthcoming.

"This needs to be discussed with the elders present," we were told, curtly.

Over the next several months, a formal investigation ensued that included meetings, interviews, and visits from leaders of the denomination. One day I even received a call from a denominational leader who asked if I was familiar with "that woman" who was leader of the church band. "You must have the wrong number," I told him. "I'm not sure who you thought you were calling, but you've reached 'that woman.'" He ended the call quickly, assuring me that we would talk again when the investigation was complete.

Of course, my first response to all of this was to quit the church. Why not? There were plenty of other churches out there, and I didn't need to deal with this crap so early in my attempt to live a life of faith, especially in light of what was happening with our family at the time. In fact, on the first Sunday after all of this happened, I fully intended to stay home and lick my wounds. But that Saturday night I felt the same hollow, too-much-swimming-pool-water feeling in my chest that I'd had on the day of my conversion. That same

> "Over the next several months, there was a formal investigation that included meetings, interviews, and visits from leaders of the denomination."

> *"That same still, small voice that told me to quit my job and sell my house said, 'Stick it out.'"*

still, small voice that told me to quit my job and sell my house said, "Stick it out." It said that I was not attending church to be served, but to serve others, and that I needed to trust God to take care of everything in his time and in his way.

This must be God, I thought, *because I just want to get the $#@& out of here.*

I had done things that had stretched me before, but this was the first time that I sensed God leading me to do something so personally challenging. Staying at this church would not be easy. Not only was I in the middle of this scandal, but as the leader of the worship band I couldn't just slip into church a little late and sit in the back and hope no one saw me. I had to stand in the front of the room and sing and play the bass, knowing that everyone was aware, with varying degrees of detail, that something was happening.

Thanks a lot, God.

I chose to point my free will in the direction of God's leading, even though I didn't want to. I stuck it out as the accusations gained momentum and word spread through the congregation. By now Pastor Thomas had chosen to stop preaching at the contemporary service while I was part of the band and an interim pastor was brought in. By church standards—by *any* standards—this was getting pretty serious.

I could not imagine why these allegations were being taken seriously, but they were. It was bizarre. To this day I am not sure exactly what the list of accusations included, since the church elders, for reasons I still do not understand, refused to share it with me. When I asked for a reason, they told me simply, "It is for your own good."

Okay, God, you won't let me leave the church, but I think threatening someone's life might be a felony in the state of New York, and since some people appear to believe this ridiculousness, maybe I should get a lawyer or contact the DA or something.

Again, after talking with Martin and some close friends, and even placing a call to a family friend who was a lawyer, the still, small voice chimed in and said, "stop." I was not to defend myself. I was to pray, stand, and serve. I wasn't supposed to leave, nor was I supposed to defend myself. I was to let my name be dragged through the mud and endure looks and whispers as people made outrageous claims against me. And I was to trust. Just trust.

Again I thought, *This must be God, because now even my old fight-or-flight instincts are getting the kibosh.*

I attended every meeting I was asked to attend, with two people by my side: Martin and a close friend from church who also happened to be a special agent for the FBI—just in case this ever went beyond the church tribunal to formal litigation.

Surprisingly, given the alleged threat, no one ever called the police.

Eventually, Pastor Thomas and his wife and their children left the church, and I was vindicated. But things never really got back to normal. That's the funny thing about gossip and false accusations. Even when the truth becomes abundantly clear, damage is often done in the telling.

I'd learned the lessons of the wave and the undertow, but what else was I supposed to learn? This was the pastor who was preaching the day of my conversion. For months he had been my main source of guidance and spiritual direction. I had

> *"That's the funny thing about gossip and false accusations. Even when the truth becomes abundantly clear, damage is often done in the telling."*

relied on him to help me, and now I was on my own.

Maybe that was it.

Without him to draw upon, I'd be forced to go directly to God and seek answers in the life of Jesus, illuminated by the Holy Spirit.

This episode might have really turned me off attending church. Could you blame me? The whole thing was just short of a witch hunt. And yet, despite all of this, I was convinced that being in community with other people of faith, and sharing and growing with them in church, was something God intended for me. I was convinced that I had to find a way to participate in church whether I liked it or not. During those months, it was as if every scripture about church found its way into my prayer and study time. Jesus is not silent on the matter. He makes clear in the scriptures that he values church. I interpreted that to mean that I didn't get to turn my back on church just because it wasn't serving my needs. I wasn't going to get to shop around for programs the way I would look for a good restaurant, and I didn't get to bad-mouth fellow churchgoers, even if they chose to snub me or tear me apart.

And most important, I learned that despite my natural tendency to do so, I couldn't just be loyal to the people I liked and hold grudges against people who harmed me. Not anymore. Not if I wanted to follow Jesus' example. Apparently, I was called to love everyone, all the time. Even when it hurts, and even when they were hurting me.

I can never be completely sure, but I think that God allowed my comfortable church existence to be shaken up so that I could

"Despite my natural tendency to do so, I couldn't just be loyal to the people I liked and hold grudges against people who harmed me. Not anymore."

learn what it means to forgive radically and to love beyond reason, even when dealing with people I would have preferred to hate.

So much for the simplicity of "Love your neighbor."

Holy Spirit Serendipity

I am going to get you a job at St. John's before I die," John whispered in my ear as I embraced him and told him how very sorry I was to hear about his diagnosis: stage IV stomach cancer.

This was the second time I had ever spoken to John. The first was about two weeks earlier, when we'd sat in a café and had a lively two-hour discussion about teaching. It was March 2007, and I was about three-quarters of the way through a master of science degree program in organizational leadership that I had begun a year earlier.

As with most big moves in my postconversion world, my return to the classroom happened quickly and without much clarity about when or even why I should do it. In the months before I signed up for the course, I was not thinking about college. Martin had finally, after several months of transitioning, closed his hardwood-flooring business. We'd taken the big step, and despite the uncertainty, we were loving our new freedom. Andrew's boarding school was finally starting to become somewhat bearable for him. It appeared that things, while still upended, might be starting to settle down a little bit.

Martin was acting in a show in Pennsylvania and took a position in a local retail store as a "day job." I spent my days writing, reading, and wondering what was next.

Returning to school for a master's degree had been on and off my radar since Andrew was born in 1989. He was barely two months old when I registered for a class at Manhattanville College, in New York. Before public relations was even a consideration, I thought teaching high school might be a good next step for a new mother. Then I learned during that first semester that I was having my second child, and the timing just didn't seem right.

I tried again in the mid-1990s, soon after marrying Martin. This time I considered an MBA, but juggling work, school, and a new marriage didn't seem to make sense. Now I found myself with the time and maybe even the desire, but I was missing two things: clarity of purpose and money for tuition.

That's when Holy Spirit serendipity stepped in.

A particular advertisement for a master's program at Nyack College, which I had never heard of, was haunting me. It seemed like I heard it on every radio station, read about it in every magazine, and saw an ad for it on every billboard. It was also in the same town as Andrew's school. *Was I supposed to go back to school?*

I wasn't sure, until a conversation with a woman I had met as part of a community volunteer program prompted me to pick up the phone and call Nyack. I decided that it couldn't hurt to call admissions to get a better idea of what we were talking about in terms of timing and money.

"This is your lucky day," the receptionist told me when I inquired about the program. "Our next cohort, which starts in eleven days, has been full for months, but we just got a call this morning and have one spot open, if you would like to consider it."

"I could see the doors opening in front of me, and I could feel an enthusiasm building—two cues that I had learned to not ignore."

Eleven days, I thought, immediately reading the coincidence as less than coincidental. *How could I possibly start school in eleven days?* Martin had just gotten settled in to his new routine. How could I hit him with this? Then there was the fact that the tuition cost was more than half the money that we had left in savings. This was another layer of crazy. And yet I could see the doors opening in front of me, and I could feel an enthusiasm building—two cues that I had learned to not ignore. I called Martin.

"Hey, Babe, I think I am supposed to spend seventeen thousand dollars and go to school." Why beat around the bush?

He was silent for a moment before he responded. There was no big push back or concern, just a simple question, "Are you sure?"

I was feeling God's leading more and more frequently, and I trusted that God was guiding my path. That said, the more I heard from God, the more I could see that there were some rogue voices intent on guiding my path as well. There was the "I want what I want when I want it" voice, and the "What? Are you crazy?" voice, and the "There is no way you can do this" voice.

This was a lot of money and neither of us was working. What if I was wrong?

I decided that I would never know if I didn't take the shot. With Martin's support, I threw my hat in the ring and prayed profusely that God would slam the door shut if this was *not* what I was meant to do.

So began the surmounting of barriers between me and graduate study.

My first job out of college had come from an internship, where they placed a far greater premium on my work ethic and ability to think on my feet than they did on my grades. From there I'd either worked hard or lucked out long enough that it was my track record, rather than my school record, that had propelled my career forward. I didn't even remember what GPA I had graduated college with, but I knew it was nothing to write home about. I couldn't imagine it was lower than the 2.5 minimum entrance requirement for the program, but I did remember that I had spent more time working to put myself through school and partying than I had worrying about grades. For me, college was all about getting the piece of paper. In the years since, I'd not thought much about what the piece of paper actually said.

Given the eleven-day deadline, pulling together my admissions package was a scramble. But by now I had some real enthusiasm for the program, and having been out of the swing of work for nearly three years, I liked the idea of going back to school, especially since the program met only once a week, for a full day on Saturdays.

Rather than wait for the mail, I drove a couple of hours up to my alma mater in Albany to grab my college transcript. It had been more than fifteen years since I had set foot in a registrar's office, and it still had the Department of Motor Vehicles feel about it. I'd brought every bit of identification and paperwork I could think of, but I still had a sense of foreboding that I wouldn't have the one piece of information I needed. Luckily, the transaction went smoothly, and in less than ten minutes I was walking out the door, transcript in hand.

Wow, I thought. *More open doors, this must be meant to be.*

I opened the envelope as I walked across the parking lot and checked the bottom right-hand corner of the paper. Cumulative average: 2.25.

And the door slammed shut.

I knew that grades had not been important to me then, but a 2.25? Ouch. This called everything into question. Nyack had been clear that 2.5 was the minimum, and I was way below it. I started to think about what to do next, but then stopped myself short. I'd prayed for God to close doors for me if this wasn't meant to be and to open doors if it was. Sure, I wanted to go to school and I was excited about the prospect, but not if it was going to throw me off track. Maybe I had gotten it wrong. If this door was closing, I had to let it close even though I had begun to get excited about returning to school. Did I trust this stuff or not?

As I considered these thoughts, that now-familiar calm came over me, and I realized that my subpar cumulative average did not matter—and ultimately, that going to school did not matter. One of two things was going to happen: they'd accept me as I was or they would not. If they did, I was meant to go to school right now. If they didn't, then this closed door would leave room for whatever I was really supposed to be

> *"If this door was closing, I had to let it close. Did I trust this stuff or not?"*

doing. Letting go of the outcome and just pressing forward made everything simple. I'd just submit the transcript and see what happened. It was liberating.

I called admissions and shared the news. There was an interview and a few more phone calls before I learned that, not only did I get in but also the admissions standards for the program were changed to accommodate returning adults like me who had significant business experience. The door opened, and I started school less than a week later.

———

I was about halfway through the program when I began to notice that I was as interested in *how* the professors were teaching as I was in the content of their lectures. I found myself observing their styles and classroom activities. I noted how one could maintain the interest of the class but others had a more difficult time. And then one morning, sitting in the Carriage Path Café, which was owned by my Aunt Karen, I blurted out to her what I had been thinking for weeks.

"I think I want to teach college."

I hadn't considered this as a possible outcome when I'd returned to school, but why not? I had more than fifteen years of business experience in communications and marketing. Now I would have an MS in organizational leadership. I had a lot to share. Why not teach?

That was when Karen told me about her friend John.

At first I wasn't sure who she was talking about as she described the white-haired man who was part of a group of guys who met for coffee a few mornings a week while I was there waiting. She pointed him out a few days later. "That's him. He's a really nice guy. Just go talk to him." And she was right.

We spent more than two hours in the Carriage Path one after-noon while he told story after story about his life before teaching and the twenty-four years he had spent at St. John's University in New York City. It didn't take long to see that he was more than just a professor. He loved his students, and he loved the school. He had been a dean at the Staten Island campus and then the director of the marketing department in the business school. As I shared my background and he shared his, there were some obvious parallels. We committed to getting together again, this time with Martin, whom John was eager to meet. I was thrilled when he said I should send him my résumé and that there might be some adjunct work for me on the Staten Island campus that fall.

A week later I walked into the café, and Karen delivered the shocking news: "Did you hear about John?" He had gone in for a test, thinking he might have an ulcer, and left with the news that he had less than a year to live.

I was floored.

I was even more floored by his committment to getting me started in teaching despite his devastating circumstances. Within weeks, he brought me to the main campus in Queens and introduced me around. Walking around the campus with John was an unbelievable experience. He knew everyone, from the janitors in the hallway to the president of the univer-sity. But he didn't just know them; he knew them by name. "Names are important," he told me, always teaching me as we walked along. He stopped and engaged everyone he met as if he or she were his best friend; no matter how serious or dis-gruntled they appeared when he first spoke to them, they re-sponded to him in kind.

True to his word, I stepped onto the Staten Island campus at St. John's for my first day of classes less than six

> *"True to his word, I stepped onto the Staten Island campus at St. John's for my first day of classes less than six months later."*

months later. I started early, a 7:35 A.M. class that necessitated leaving home at 4:30 A.M. to ensure that I missed traffic and got there on time. But I didn't mind. I was grateful for the opportunity, and I was willing to pay my dues. I took a few moments before my first class to sit outside, under the trees at a small black metal café table, beside the cream-colored stucco building that was more reminiscent of Italy than of Staten Island. I wrote about gratitude and the amazing road that had led me to teaching. Moments later, confident but cautious, I stepped into my first classroom as Professor Ball.

I couldn't have done it without the mentoring and friendship that John had showed me in the months between our meeting and his death a year later. Ever the marketing professor, he taught me that teaching was about customer service and that these eighteen-, nineteen-, and twenty-year-old students were my customers. "It is not about knowing everything and dispensing wisdom from on high," he told me. "It is about reaching each student individually, heart to heart. It is about connecting with them as human beings in a way that meets their needs, not your convenience."

Simple wisdom that applies in and out of the classroom.

John's death was a sad day for many people. I sat with a good friend of his at the memorial mass, which filled to capacity the church on the Queens campus of the university. The Catholic priests talked about his commitment to St. John's and his commitment to his students. Dozens of current and former students attended. One overarching theme was made clear by each speaker: John loved his students and colleagues demonstrably, and he had made a difference in their lives. His life was an example of the tremendous power of one individual to touch the lives of many. In addition to paving the way for me to teach—a new vocation I am very grateful for—he taught me valuable lessons about dealing with people, something I have struggled with my whole life. John's gift for radiating love and care to others inspired in me the deep desire to learn to do likewise.

Mary and the Monks

The only noise was the distant purr of a four-wheel-drive truck with a plow on the front doing its best to tame the nearly two feet of snow that had fallen, while trying to keep ahead of a skyful that hadn't yet reached ground. I chose this room specifically for its two bright windows on an exposed brick wall and the small desk that sidled up next to the radiator. Some might think the room too small or too warm, but for me it was just perfect.

I had arrived a couple of days earlier, on Friday, December 19, 2008, ready to put a cap on the year that had both devastated and delighted me more than any I had endured since coming to faith in 2003. The roads had a light dusting of snow and were just hinting at how slippery they would become as I turned my little red Scion into the sloped drive, passing the now familiar burgundy sign that read HOLY CROSS MONASTERY.

Holy Cross is an Episcopal monastery in the Benedictine tradition, one of half a dozen Catholic and Protestant monasteries on this stretch of road that runs parallel to the Hudson

River about two hours north of New York City. It has also become, without intention, the first place I have found since my conversion that I would consider calling my spiritual home. I've tried more than once to recall how it was that I found this place, and while the practical answer is "on the Internet," I am confident that "happenstance" does not get to the heart of it. As with so many of these lily pads that I have hopped onto, one by one across this pond of conversion, faith, and life, I have found that those parts of the journey that were most profound are the ones that I have the hardest time recalling in concrete terms. In the same way that I hadn't set out to find this faith, I did not set out to find a monastery, a spiritual guide, or a spiritual home. But somehow, at Holy Cross, I found all three.

My first visits were short and began as part of a pattern of weekly Sabbath rests that I had initiated for a year in 2006. I would arrive in the morning, wander around grounds that stretched downhill across a broad meadow from the four-story brick guesthouse, to a border swath of forest that curled like ribbon trim along the river's edge. A well-worn foot trail, peppered with small piles of sticks and stones left by pilgrims and seekers who had passed that way before, wound through the trees, zigzagging downward to the edge of the water. A tire swing hung in a small clearing where I liked to sit and write among the smooth rounded river stones and uprooted trees that washed up onto the shore. I laughed out loud the first time I saw the swing, picturing the monks flying out over the water, full white vestments flapping behind them in the breeze.

Stop it, Joan, I repriman-
ded myself, looking around
as if someone might hear
my unspoken thoughts. *That
kind of thinking must be some
brand of sin.*

"I pictured the monks flying out over the water, full white vestments flapping behind them in the breeze."

It was a month or two
later that I responded to a
posting on the monastery
Web site about a five-day silent retreat. I'd never been on a
retreat before, silent or not. I was understandably concerned
when the woman who checked me into the guesthouse
looked at me askance and said, "Boy, you are really jumping
in with two feet," when I told her that I was both a new
Christian and that I'd never done anything like this before. At
that time I didn't know enough about silence or retreats to
understand what she meant.

She assigned me a room, which had the name of a saint
rather than a number, and I walked out to my car to grab my
bags. It pains me to recall my opening the hatch of the car to
drag out two suitcases, one for clothing and the other for toi-
letries and the eight pairs of shoes I'd convinced myself I had
to bring—just in case. I was like a character in a bad sitcom,
dressed to the nines with makeup and accessories, a fish out of
water in the relaxed environment of the monastery.

And yet, I learned quickly that silence suited me, and I
adapted to the gentle rhythm of the place. Four spiritual
directors—a lovely older couple who looked straight out of a
British parlor; a tall, regal-looking nun from the order of St.
Helena's; and an Episcopal priest with bright red hair and a
generous smile—gathered the retreatants and explained how
our stay was going to work.

"How many of you have been on a silent retreat before?" the elder gentleman with white hair asked. Everyone but me lifted a hand. I could have been uncomfortable, but for some reason I wasn't. I just listened as they described how things were going to work.

"Silence involves more than just refraining from talking," he explained. "Reading, writing, even nodding politely to one another in the hallway can break silence." While I knew that body language was an important aspect of communication, I had never considered limiting it when observing silence. And truthfully, I had never considered observing silence like this before. I was intrigued.

"You will have the opportunity to meet one-on-one with a spiritual director, who will check in with you to see how things are going, for forty-five minutes each day," the gentleman's wife continued. "Otherwise, you are free to come and go as you please and to attend the fixed-hour services, Matins at 7:00 A.M., Holy Eucharist at 8:30 A.M., Diurnum at noon, Vespers at 5:00 P.M., and Compline at 7:30 P.M."

It took me two and a half days to come to a place where my head was not racing with thoughts and I could comfortably claim to be in silence. It was wonderful. The tempo of the days at Holy Cross, the bells that were rung to announce meals and prayer times, the crypt in the basement filled with art and space to sit quietly—I loved all of it. By the time I left, I was downright embarrassed to walk out with my big bags and all those shoes. What had I been thinking?

But then, recognizing that I needed to be gentle with myself, I recalled that the simple answer was that I wasn't thinking. This was just another go-and-see stop on my ragtag journey. I had made myself present and was ready for anything. I just hadn't yet learned that, in God's economy, being

ready for anything had more
to do with what was in my
heart than what was on my
feet.

I returned to Holy
Cross several times between
2006 and 2008, which was
when I met a brother with
whom I began to meet reg-

*"It took me two and a half days to
come to a place where my head was
not racing with thoughts and I could
comfortably claim to be in silence."*

ularly for spiritual direction. Brother Bernard is Belgian by
birth. He spent years as an investment banker for J.P. Morgan
before joining the Order of the Holy Cross. He also commu-
nicates with his family in Europe on Skype, is an active blogger, and once sent me a "What Saint Are You?" quiz on
Facebook—talk about bridging the ancient-modern gap.

On this visit in December 2008, I was planning to stay
until Tuesday, the day before Christmas Eve. In some ways,
leaving my family to write for nearly a week before Christmas
seemed positively decadent. I should have been home buying
gifts or wrapping presents or caroling or doing something else
suitably Christmasy, but this was no ordinary Christmas. The
wave had crested and the undertow pulled me down that
year, leaving me to spin in the wake of a tsunami of joy and
heartbreak as the year came to a close. These days leading
into 2009 offered me time to focus on the blessings that were
shaping my future and a flood of heartache that had con-
sumed my recent past.

The year had begun with the news that my mother's
kidney cancer, which she had been fighting for several years,

was finally getting the better of her. While you wouldn't have known it to see her getting dressed and putting on her jewelry for radiation treatments, her long silences were beginning to say more than any words could. It had become an unspoken truth: we would not see another Christmas with my mother.

My siblings, my father, her siblings, and her family friends surrounded her, day in and day out, as we tried to make her as comfortable as possible. There are many stories I could tell about my mother and her strength and dignity in the face of her illness. She was a nurse, so she knew the enemy she faced, and she did it with grace and elegance. While I would love to paint a beautiful picture of my mother's life, the time for that story is not now; I am just not ready. You see, in addition to losing my sixty-five-year-old mother in April 2008, without warning—three weeks before she passed away—she lost her husband of forty-six years, my father, to a stroke at age sixty-seven.

I'm sorry to hear about your dad, Professor Ball," one of my students, I will call her Julie, said as I packed my bag to head home. I was finishing my first year of teaching at St. John's, knowing that I would be canceling class for my father's funeral two days later, so I decided to drive in and get the kids settled before finals week.

"Thank you, honey," I said, barely registering my response.

Julie continued, telling me that she had lost her father when she was twelve and that it was hard for a long time, but that healing eventually came. She spoke as one who had been living as an adult longer than her twenty years would indicate.

"You will never forget him," she said to me.

That was true. My father's vision of what I could be was one of the sources of my courage and determination, even as it challenged me over the years. A host of conflicting memories and emotions churned in my mind as my thoughts turned back to Julie.

I had come to know a little bit of this student's story, having taught her the previous semester as well. She was a real go-getter who had not only put herself through college but also was living with her boyfriend and actively helping him raise his young children, ages two and four. Several months earlier she had missed a couple of classes to testify in court as part of a custody battle; the mother of her boyfriend's children was hoping to take them out of state. She and her boyfriend eventually lost custody, and they were planning to move to be near the children, as soon as she graduated in May.

"Thanks, Julie," I said as I continued packing my bag. I'll admit that I only half acknowledged her kind words. I had already switched gears, focusing on completing my last review session before heading out to help make photo collages for the wake or whatever last-minute prep needed to be done for my father's funeral.

As I drove home a couple of hours later, my cell phone rang. It was Julie. She was sobbing so hard that I could hardly make out what she was saying.

"What is it? What happened?" While I usually had a very high threshold for the latest student drama, this was not the day for it. My students sometimes tended to overdramatize ordinary events, especially when they were trying to take off on the day of a test, so I was ready for anything. What came next was no typical student drama.

> " 'The baby drowned,' she was wailing. 'They are trying to save her now. I knew something like this would happen.'"

"The baby drowned," she was wailing. "They are trying to save her now. I knew something like this would happen." Apparently the younger of her boyfriend's two children had drowned in her mother's backyard swimming pool.

My heart sank.

"Julie, listen to me. I need you to calm down. Where are you? Where is your boyfriend? What are you doing now?" I was already operating in crisis mode, so it was not difficult for me to calm her down and get her to listen. "You don't have enough information yet," I told her. "Take a deep breath, try to compose yourself, and get to where your boyfriend is. That is all you can do right now. The rest is out of your hands."

She left me a voicemail the next day, her voice devoid of emotion. "She didn't make it, Professor Ball." The baby was two years old. Julie didn't leave a phone number, so I couldn't call her back. Then, again, maybe it was better that way. I needed to be with my family, and she needed to be with hers.

Julie showed up at the end of class the following Tuesday and explained what had transpired. We sat quietly, commiserating without saying a word.

I am still numb as I write this. While I know that the time will come when I will thoroughly explore the spiritual questions that arise from the deaths of my parents and John and that little girl within months of one another, right now, the losses are still too close for me to have gained the perspective that comes with the passing of time. For some reason, rather than shaking my faith, the challenges of 2008 and the years that preceded it helped me see how important and precious this faith is to me. I cannot imagine what I would have done without it. I can't explain why I have not, like many people do, blamed God or turned my back on him as a result of these events—but the thought never crossed my mind. On the contrary. I find myself drawing in close and taking comfort in his presence as he walks it out with me.

That Sunday in December at Holy Cross, as I reached some deadline on my manuscript and prepared to return home to face a Christmas season that felt less than joyful, I sensed God's wink via a sermon given by one of the monks, Brother Robert. I'd never met him, nor did he know a thing about me. Yet, he spoke directly to my heart that morning, giving me a succinct context for all I had endured and all that was yet to come in a way that only God can choreograph.

He stepped to a wooden dais in the middle of the chapel, greeted his brothers and the seated guests, and began:

This morning at 7:04 A.M., at just about the time we were finishing the recitation of the *Venite* here in the chapel and repeating its lovely antiphon, *Our King and Savior now draws near, Come let us worship. Alleluia,* we were experiencing an astronomical event, though most of us were quite likely unaware of it. It was, of course, the moment of the winter solstice, that point in the yearly cycle of our solar system when (at least in our Northern Hemisphere) the sun's path reaches its lowest and most northward arc across the skies. The night is at its longest, the day is at its shortest and everything seems to come to a stop or a complete halt.

That's the literal meaning of the word *solstice*—the sun stopping—reminiscent of what Joshua (or more accurately, God) accomplished. Or what any ordinary swimmer swimming laps or runner running an old-fashioned relay must do before reversing directions. He or she must come to a complete stop, if only for a nanosecond, before turning around and returning home. St. Basil tells us that this is a wonderful image of the path of conversion. Like the sun in the heavens or the Prodigal Son in the Gospel, we must all at some point stop before we can reverse the direction of our lives.

And it's often this very simple but critical act of stopping which is most difficult and most unavailable to us. Can't we just keep on going? But as much as we would wish otherwise, life is in fact radically discontinuous. It is punctuated by repeated moments of stopping, of braking, of reversal, and of change, more often like a quantum leap than a smooth bell curve. It can feel that way with the times and seasons of our lives.

Welcome winter!

So much of our celebration of the Advent season and of Christmas is shaped culturally by this astronomical occurrence of the winter solstice, with its ready-made natural symbols of life and death, darkness and light, cold and warmth, activity and quiet that we associate with these days . . . not to mention the secular overlay of snowmen, elves, evergreens, holly, poinsettias, food, and gift-giving—the latter two obviously more deeply symbolic and sacramental than, say, Frosty or the Little Drummer Boy.

I would hope [our celebration] might go right back to this very familiar passage from St. Luke's Gospel read this morning throughout the Christian world, back to this wonderful, mystic, mythic, layered, compelling, gentle story of the Annunciation which informs our theology and shapes our devotional and spiritual lives in ways that are both insistent and subtle.

A woman, an angel, a pregnancy . . . a mystery. It's pretty primal stuff, just like that related story of the woman, the serpent, and the tree. Perhaps the most insistent and subtle way this shaping or formation happens for us—or at least for me—is the practice we have in the monastery of ringing the Angelus three times a day, calling to mind today's Gospel story.

It is admittedly not an ancient practice—perhaps five or six hundred years old—but there is a certain timelessness to it. If it didn't exist, we might be forced to invent it. All of us here are familiar with the practice. Three times a day—morning, midday, and evening—we chime the tower bell in a rather complicated set of three sets of three followed by nine. And as we also know, there are certain traditional texts connected to the ringing:

> *"The angel of the Lord brought tidings to Mary, and she*
> *conceived by the Holy Spirit."*
> *"Mary said: Behold I am the servant of the Lord; let it be*
> *to me according to your word."*
> *"The Word was made flesh and dwelt among us."*

I love this devotion, this practice, this Angelus, because it invites me, wherever I may be, whatever I may be doing, to stop and recall that there is always a bigger picture and a larger setting than my often very narrow concerns allow. It is a reminder, a regular and (for me) necessary reminder, that God is God and I am not. I might add that I was fortunate to grow up in a city where there were many, many Catholic churches in my neighborhood and so at noon and 6:00 P.M. and yes, even at 6:00 A.M., there was a veritable choir of bells for miles around calling me to this awareness long before I could ever articulate it.

I love this practice because it daily reminds me of the epic sweep of our salvation history: It reminds me of Mary, the daughter descended from King David, through whom we look back to our primal parents and our Jewish heritage. It reminds me Jesus, the eternal Word, and Power of God come among us in the flesh. It reminds me of the continuing, loving, saving action of God available and effective in a broken and desperate world. Who of us doesn't need to be reminded of that daily, even hourly?

But most of all I love the Angelus because it presents *in the simplest possible terms* the fundamental shape of Christian life. One of my fellow novices, the late Gary Mattson, pointed this out to me years ago, and I have never forgotten it. The structure is always the same: Annunciation, Response, Incarnation. That's how it happens, over and over again. That's how it happens to us, to all people. God invites, suggests, encourages, perhaps even commands. We jump at the opportunity or perhaps more realistically, drag our feet, ask our questions, consider the costs, and maybe squirm a bit. But ultimately if we are wise, if we are graced, if we're lucky, we give our consent, and with Mary, we say yes. Then the real mystery happens: God takes on flesh once again, in ways big and small, in ways predictable or stunning, in places most necessary and perhaps most feared. But the pattern is always the same: Annunciation, Response, Incarnation. It's good to remember when the way appears dim and the going gets rough and life seems complex, because it is.

It's also good to remember that for most of us, most of the time, the consent asked of us is to small and ordinary acts of faithfulness: the invitation to trust in this circumstance that God will be faithful; the decision to act not out of fear or suspicion but out of hope; the possibility of risking to be vulnerable with this brother or sister; this opportunity of forgiving or accepting that we are ourselves forgiven; the willingness to fall, to fail, or to be proven the fool because that's where God seems to be inviting us. Today. Every day. Here we are, huddled together on this cold and snowy fourth Sunday of Advent, on the shortest day of the year, invited once again by God. To what? To wait. To hope. To trust. To act. To love. To share. To be just. To just be.

What is it that God is inviting you or me to this morning? What is the Annunciation, the suggestion, the command, the dream today? And how shall we respond? How shall Christ become flesh again in our midst? In our community? In our society? In our hearts?

Brother Robert's sermon asked the questions I needed to consider before heading home for what was sure to be a difficult Christmas. The same questions a life of faith requires me to ask and answer every day.

Commitment

It is January 2009, and I'm bent over a thick stew of shoes piled in the bottom of my closet, hovering precariously on one bare leg with the other clothed in a brown, knee-high, three-and-a-half-inch heeled leather boot.

"Where is it?" I wasn't quite sure if my exasperated mutter was in my head, under my breath, or full voice.

"What are you looking for?" came Martin's answer.

I could tell by his tone that I'd not only given voice to my frustration but also made it abundantly clear that the missing boot was getting the better of me. As I continued to sift through mismatched footwear, my inner compass was working overtime. Somewhere behind my sternum the voice of reason was tapping out rapid-fire Morse code messages to my brain.

Stop . . . Abort . . . This is no way to start your day . . . especially over a boot.

I was off balance in more ways than one. I knew that the boot wasn't the real source of my frustration. This was about the disarray. It was about another inconvenience resulting from another lost battle in the commit-to-change versus fail-to-change war I'd been fighting with several bad habits—including my tendency to leave clothes, shoes, books, and other gear strewn haphazardly in my wake. I am fully aware that there are worse vices than being a slob. And admittedly, I've embraced and subsequently kicked many of those vices in my day. But this seemingly mundane discipline stuff was beginning to appear unbeatable. And I was sick of it.

In the years before the Creator of the Universe knocked my legs out from under me, my motivation for self-improvement had been primarily selfish. I used to think how much easier life would be if there were a place for everything and everything was in its place. No more lost keys. No last-minute ironing pulled from the bottom of a pile of clean (or sometimes dirty) laundry before I ran out the door, late for whatever. Of course, back then I also had the money to hire people to pick up the slack where my less than organized nature left off. But now, standing in front of that closet with more than five years in the Christian trenches and no money in the bank for the mortgage, not to mention a housekeeper, I'd learned (mostly the hard way) that my things are a gift and that treating the nouns in my life with respect is an expression of gratitude to the Giver. Unfortunately, that meant that shooting dirty looks at Martin and kicking shoes around my bedroom were an expression of something else.

> "I'd learned (mostly the hard way) that treating the nouns in my life with respect is an expression of gratitude to the Giver."

What I hadn't yet grasped was that this budding tantrum ran deeper than the mislaid boot or the disarray. Sure, both were annoying. But they were mere hints of a long-time foe that I'd begun to fight in recovery in the mid-1990s, and that I continued to battle with some new allies since that June day in 2003. Like a master of disguise, this subtle enemy shows up and does its damage before I even know it's there. Lurking in the back of my mind and in the depths of my heart, it comes like a wolf in sheep's clothing, twisting the truth just enough to appear welcome. The foe was this: there was and always would be a chasm between what I hope to do and what I actually do.

No matter how devoted I am to this new life, I am never going to be perfect, and sometimes, even though I know it is not right, that really sets me off. Perhaps that's why humility is so central to both a life in recovery and a life of faith. On those once rare but now increasingly common days that I fully recognize where I fit in the world—my right size—that desire to be perfect or to pursue "arriving" becomes a valid lifelong journey rather than an intense and unreachable daily goal. When I'm living in *that* reality, it is much easier for me to have a sense of humor about daily annoyances, like missing boots. When I am living in the *other* reality, though—the one in which I actually believe that I can and should do everything right all the time—that's when I allow unrealistic expectations to send me through the roof. Of course, I know all of this. But standing there in front of my closet, I couldn't see past my adolescent I-want-what-I-want-when-I-want-it attitude. Turning to Martin with the intention of snapping at him for having the audacity to try to help me, I instead watched him cross the room and, like a living, breathing metaphor, flip on the overhead light.

I was actually startled. In my self-imposed mayhem, I hadn't noticed that I'd mounted the mad search for my boot in the dim light of an overcast morning, through cream-colored linen curtains with just enough light to see but not enough light to find. Looking back down into the closet, I could immediately make out a dime-size square of brown leather the length of which I followed through pumps, sneakers, flats, and chunky slippers to a gold-colored buckle peeking out from behind a pair of gaudy faux-leather cowboy boots. The lost boot had been recovered.

"Thanks, Babe," I said to Martin, shooting the half smile that adds an automatic, *I'm sorry, I know I am a brat*, to whatever I just said. "No problem," he smiled back, climbing over a pile of my clothes to get to his neat, well-organized closet. Thankfully this was one of those mornings when my inner adolescent met his inner adult, and we were able to immediately start over. I'd need a whole separate chapter to tell you how it might have gone if it had been one of those adolescent-on-adolescent mornings.

During my years in recovery I had frequently heard and attempted to live the slogan, "Progress, Not Perfection." In the years since my experience in 2003, I've come to learn a similar, liberating truth about the myth of Christian perfection. It is just that, a myth.

Both recovery and Christian faith, when operating at their best, acknowledge the paradox between journey and arrival, between taking action and letting go. Addicts become sober and they have to work hard to let go in order to stay that way. Christians come to faith and must work hard to let go in order to grow in faith. At least, that's how it has worked for me. It sounds like it should be easy, but working hard to stop working so hard can be the hardest work of all.

When I first set out on this journey, I read and listened and watched and attended conferences. I wanted to learn everything. Nothing inherently wrong with that, I suppose. I think God likes it when we try to get to know him better. And yet, with all of the wisdom and knowledge and tactics and suggestions, none of it seems to have relieved me permanently from being a brat sometimes when I don't get my way.

"Working hard to stop working so hard can be the hardest work of all."

So why, given this apparent lack of progress, should I bother? Why should anyone bother?

That morning, as I shook off my near meltdown and set out to get on with my day, something occurred to me. After years of fighting my humanity, I had, for a moment when that light came on in that room, been able to see through both the mess in my closet and the mess in myself, and to just accept. Sometimes I'm a slob and sometimes I am a brat. But, ultimately, I am a work in progress—and that is okay. This might be intuitive for some people, but I am one of those who have spent most of their adult lives unable to admit these things.

Some combination of self-consciousness, self-protection, and self-deception—demons I have been fighting for as long as I can remember—kept me from sharing the truth about myself with anyone, including myself. I was an expert at keeping my weaknesses under wraps—until they popped up in unintended and unexpected places. That's when, as an act of protection, I would defend them, blame them on others, or recast them as virtues and wear them as a badge of distinction.

So, no, I have not arrived. But through the transforming strength of this higher power, this God, this Jesus, this Holy

Spirit of God, I am coming to a more genuine understanding of myself. I am increasingly willing to allow Divine light to have access to the deepest, darkest, and most broken parts of myself, and allow it to do its transforming work on my heart, my soul, and my mind.

As God continues to work on who I am on the inside, things have begun to change on the outside. Many of the things that we had been hoping and praying for have begun to happen, although some have come in odd packages. I signed my first book contract and was offered a full-time teaching position. Hooked on teaching and hoping to make it a second career, I am now pursuing my PhD.

Martin broke his arm before a big show, which put his acting on hold, but he spent the time that he would have been performing creating some interesting mixed-media art instead. Since then he has had several gallery shows, and a French curator and artist just took some of his pieces back to France to exhibit in his gallery. He has also returned to his roots, performing and writing Spanish music, and is enrolled in college, studying graphic design.

Andrew is healthy and happy, attending college and living in an apartment with a bunch of friends. He hopes to help young people who struggle with neurological issues. Kelsey is finding herself and studying music production; Ian is a happy little eleven-year-old who doesn't even remember that I used to work in corporate.

After a lifetime of operating at a distance from people—either physically or emotionally—something has broken in me and allowed me to connect with God and with other people in a way I never imagined was possible. It was this connection that I was looking for when I was a little kid, lying to be part of the crowd. It was this connection I had sought, and not been able to find, when I dabbled in faith and tried to escape with drink and drugs all of those years ago. It is the connection I gave up when I decided that I could go it alone and be the master of my destiny through my twenties. It is

"I am not flirting with faith anymore. I've finally made a commitment, once and for all. For better or for worse. For richer, for poorer. In sickness and in health."

the connection I nearly abandoned when I brought my arrogance with me into faith and became a know-it-all rather than a love-it-all Christian in those first years of rules-based practice. It is the kind of connection, rooted in radical love and radical faith, that I had flirted with my whole life but never grasped until, in progressive acts of pure grace, God gave me these opportunities to see the truth of my own self-deception and turn myself around.

I am not flirting with faith anymore. I've finally made a commitment, once and for all. For better or for worse. For richer, for poorer. In sickness and in health. I plan to follow this countercultural adventure with God wherever it takes me. Pressing forward and committed in times of joy and times of trial, as long as we both shall live.

ABOUT THE AUTHOR

Joan Ball spent more than fifteen years in the public-relations business before making the transition from the boardroom to the classroom in 2007. She currently teaches marketing in the Peter J. Tobin College of Business at St. John's University in Queens, New York, and writes for Beliefnet.com. A media-relations expert, she has been the corporate spokesperson for a variety of large and midsize professional-services firms. Central to her story is the extent to which she allowed her career and the money, prestige, and possessions that came with it to overshadow the things that were most important in life. In *Flirting with Faith,* she shares with bold candor both her challenges and successes—from single motherhood to alcohol addiction to unbalanced priorities in the midst of apparent accomplishment—with transparency and openness. She and her husband, Martin, live in suburban New York with their son Ian. Her adult children, Kelsey (twenty) and Andrew (twenty-one) are undergraduate students elsewhere in New York.

No one—least of all herself—expected Joan Ball to become a follower of Jesus. *Flirting with Faith* is the story of how she comes to embrace a spiritual way of living. Told with candor and humor, Joan's story is intimate yet surprisingly universal. As she begins to develop a new spiritual lifestyle and nourish her deepening faith, Joan embarks on a humbling, exhilarating journey that will have readers—both skeptical and devout —reexamining their relationship with the Divine.

DISCUSSION QUESTIONS

1. Joan has a sudden and profound spiritual experience while sitting in church with her family. This preliminary spiritual awakening is so intense that she initially thinks she is having a heart attack. Can you relate to Joan's experience? Why do you think her awakening was so sudden and powerful?

2. Before being "struck" Christian, Joan thought organized religion was a burden and unnecessary to live a complete life. Consider your own religious views: do the benefits of religious living outweigh those of an atheistic or agnostic lifestyle, or vice versa? Have your views on faith and religion changed now that you have read *Flirting with Faith*?

3. As she reflects on her conversion, Joan writes that "this unlikely encounter with the Divine relieved me of the luxury of unbelief" (page 30). In your opinion, is unbelief a luxury? What makes belief or disbelief in God, the Divine, or the Holy Spirit luxurious?

4. When describing her years in college, Joan notes that her interest in faith manifested while she was living with her free-spirited roommate Darcy. If Joan had never investigated spirituality, do you think her story would have followed the same course, or do you think her spiritual awakening might have happened differently?

5. Long before being reborn as a Christian, Joan explored spirituality through a variety of mediums: in books, with spiritual practices like meditation, with crystals, and in the I Ching. She then spent seven years pursuing a relationship with a power-greater-than-herself in addiction recovery. What spiritual options have you explored? Did you have any successes or failures with these attempts?

6. Most of the other Christians Joan interacts with throughout her story were raised Christian or eased into Christian faith with little difficulty, which sometimes made her feel like a "spiritual oddball" (page 55). Do you think that Joan's spiritual path is particularly odd? What about her story is unique? What about her story is universal?

7. Often throughout her narrative, Joan infers that God must be working in her life, for her prideful, rational mind would have never entertained acting against her own desires as she did when leaving her career, selling her possessions and moving from her dream house. Do you think

you can have a spiritual awakening without this sort of a psychic redirection? Should living a life of faith include constant changes in thinking patterns and behaviors?

8. Joan takes on a number of spiritual mentors. Her first teacher is Pastor Thomas, who claims "Many people who come to faith have an enthusiasm for sharing it with others, [which] is a good thing. Nothing to worry about" (page 89). What do you think: Is belief meant to be shared with others? Or should it be enjoyed on your own? Do you have a spiritual mentor?

9. Joan offers insight into her personal history, including her alcoholism and drug abuse and the seven years in addiction recovery that preceded her conversion to Christianity. Compare Joan's lifestyle during each of these periods (specifically her behavior detailed in Chapter 11, "Illusion of Control"). In what ways do they differ? Are there any similarities? Does her conversion result in a complete moral and attitudinal change, or do you think it will be an ongoing process?

10. "Skydiving in the Nude" details not only Joan's increasing faith in God's arrangements but also her husband, Martin's, proclivity for living out his faith more deeply. As Joan shares her burgeoning faith with Martin, he in turn begins to trust more in God's plans for him and his family. Compare your own faith-based relationships and experiences with Joan's. Do you think one person's advancing faith can promote spiritual hunger in another person?

11. Once Martin decides to pursue a career in acting, Joan completely supports his decision. She writes "I stood qui-

etly watching him as he wrestled with himself. I prayed without speaking . . . It was not lost on me that I was, in effect, praying for financial instability" (page 151). Here we see Joan sacrificing her own needs for the spiritual growth and benefit of others. Do you think this is a foolish or wise choice? Do you think her selflessness nourishes her advancing faith?

12. The final chapters find Joan dealing with extremely difficult challenges to her faith: both she and her husband begin new careers; her son Andrew suffers from a severe illness; she even finds controversy in her church when another person falsely accuses her of criminal intentions. "It seemed like the more we tried to follow God and do what we perceived we were supposed to do, the more difficult and unpredictable things became" (page 161). Still, her faith never wavers. Is it more or less difficult to be faithful in times of struggle?

13. Although Joan experiences many moments of spiritual uplift, she also wades through times of great despair. Do you think that anyone is capable of complete, ongoing spiritual clarity? What do you think makes a successful spiritual life?

14. Despite her newfound calmness and trust in God's plan, the personality Joan exhibited before her conversion still pops up. This is especially evident in her confrontations with Pastor Thomas regarding accusations made against Joan. What do you think about the instances where Joan lapses into her preconversion attitudes?

ENHANCING YOUR BOOK CLUB

1. Reread Chapter 8, "Wide Awake." During the first months after her conversion, Joan spent plenty of time studying the Bible. Flipping between chapters and verses, she begins to notice parallels not only within the text but between the Bible's stories and her own life, both her current and former way of living. She comes to call this practice "spiritual calisthenics" (page 76). Give Joan's exercise a try. Skim through random passages of the Bible and see if you notice any patterns. Can you relate to certain verses more than others? Journal on your experience and share it with your friends.

2. In addition to the Bible and other Christian literature, Joan reads many spiritual texts on her journey. Examples include the Bhagavad Gita, Ayn Rand's *The Fountainhead*, Julia Cameron's *The Artist's Way*, and others. Read some or all of these texts. Are there any parallels between these books and *Flirting with Faith*? Are there any other books you think Joan would've enjoyed or learned from in her early days as a new Christian?

3. Joan finds religious comfort in many other places outside of church: at the beach, at a monastery, in temples, even in coffee shops. Spend an afternoon or a day exploring different locations you think might promote spiritual calmness. Where are some of these places? Is there one you prefer more than others?

QUESTIONS FOR THE AUTHOR

1. What compelled you to write *Flirting with Faith?*

Flirting with Faith was not my first book idea. I had written a proposal for a book called *From Debate to Dialog: Bridging the Spiritual Communication Gap* that included a rather self-righteous treatise on the ills of self-righteousness. I was completely unaware of the hypocrisy of the organized-religion-has-it-wrong-but-I-have-it-right posture I'd taken in that first proposal until I was told that it "felt like someone was wagging a finger" at the reader. Once I recovered from the bruising to my ego, I became curious about this apparent blind spot and decided to stop writing for publication until I could better understand the disconnect between my desire to share the story of my faith and my impulse to condescend. After eighteen months of soul-searching I began writing again, and *Flirting with Faith* was the result.

2. You plumb some harrowing moments in your life, both pre- and post-conversion. Were any particularly difficult to revisit?

I have said more than once that the years following my conversion to Christianity have been some of the most wonderful and most difficult in my life. Revisiting the challenges we've faced since 2003 and the years I spent as a single mother in the 1990s was both difficult and cleansing. I am sure I have more depths to plumb as I continue forward as a writer.

3. Did you learn anything new about yourself while writing this book?

I'm not sure if it is new or just a confirmation that I have a tendency to be a perfectionist. While this might appear to be a virtue, perfectionism can hamper creativity. I wonder how my writing will change as I continue to learn to let go and let God.

4. You go into great detail about specific moments and experiences during your first years as a new Christian. How did you recall these instances? Did you utilize journals or other artifacts to remember the specificities of these memories?

In the months and years following my conversion I filled dozens of journals and notebooks with thoughts, reflections, prayers, and questions. I initially thought I would reread all forty-plus of them prior to writing the book, but things did not evolve that way. Instead I would recall a situation and find a journal that covered that time period. Some day I would love to take them to a little house by the ocean and read them all cover to cover. I'm guessing there are some more interesting stories in there.

5. Because this is a work of nonfiction, the reader can infer that the other people who populate your story are not constructions but flesh-and-blood persons who you know personally, like your husband and your various

mentors. Were you afraid that these people would not like how they are portrayed in *Flirting with Faith*?

I did my best to respect the privacy of the people I write about in this book. Names are changed in some cases, and details (especially regarding my children) are kept to a minimum. I did my best to get things right, including giving early drafts to my family and people who lived through circumstances with me to make sure I wasn't missing anything. That said, I am sure there will be people who are made uncomfortable by my story and the parts they played in it. I'll have to cross those bridges when I come to them.

6. In the last few years there seems to have been a resurgence of spiritual memoirs and tales of people seeking religious guidance. What do you think this says about our current social and moral climate?

I think that we are living in a very complicated society at a very complicated time in our history. Rapid changes in the way people live and communicate with one another are resulting in us being both more and less connected than ever. Postmodernism and the propensity for relativism challenges traditional concepts of faith, morality, and virtue in a way that raises a lot of questions, and people, rather than keeping quiet, are asking them. I hope that this book becomes part of that conversation.

7. The ending of *Flirting with Faith* is exceptionally even-handed. Rather than supply an overly optimistic finale,

you close with a complete transcript of Brother Robert's speech and hopeful reflections on the difficulties and joys of religious living. What message were you hoping to convey with this conclusion?

I'm not sure I had a particular message in mind other than it being an honest assessment of where I am on this faith journey. The story of my experience with God does not create a pristine Hollywood arc: girl meets God and everything ends happily ever after. This is a process, a commitment, and I am still unclear about exactly where all of this is taking me. The best I can do is listen and try to do the next right thing.

8. You do not shy away from sharing with readers your moments of doubt and confusion about religion and God. What advice would you offer to people who might be experiencing similar struggles? Are there any particular methods you found healing or that alleviated extreme doubt?

The best advice I could give someone who is confused or in doubt is to allow themselves to stay there, rather than attempting to take steps to make it go away (such as pretending to believe or hastily abandoning faith to return to comfortable answers). The doubt, confusion, and uncertainty are part of the process and there is much to be learned by pressing through them in pursuit of a deeper understanding of God.

9. You've made serious lifestyle changes during the course of your life. Not only have you embraced a Christian way

of life but you've battled alcoholism, changed career paths multiple times, and even uprooted your family from your home. Do you wish any of these events turned out differently? Do you regret any of the paths you've followed on your spiritual journey?

If I regret any of it, I would have to regret all of it, since I needed to live every moment of the life I have lived to become the woman I am today.

10. How has your faith grown now that you've completed *Flirting with Faith*? Have your beliefs changed in any way?

My faith grows and changes every day. I recently had some experiences that are pointing me in the direction of my next book. I learned so much and changed so much in the process of living and writing this book, so I am confident that even more will be revealed.

WITHDRAWAL

4c - 6/
11/12-3

**Indianapolis
Marion County
Public Library**

Renew by Phone
269-5222

Renew on the Web
www.imcpl.org

For General Library Information
please call 269-1700

DEMCO